Unknown Bodies:

Mothers Daughters and Adoption

a memoir

Janine M. Veto

5346 Coney Weston Place
Madison, Wisconsin 53711

Portions of this book first appeared in somewhat different form in *Confrontation* magazine, No. 80/81, Martin Tucker, ed., C.W. Post of Long Island University, New York, 2002/2003; *Fine China, Earth's Daughters*/Springhouse Editions, New York, 1993; *The Dream Book,* Helen Barolini, ed., Schocken Books, New York, 1985, 1987; *la bella figura*, Rose Romano, ed., San Francisco, 1989.

Names of some of the parties in this book have been changed.

Photograph on page 106 courtesy of Nancy Crampton. All other photographs from the author's private collection.

ISBN 978-1-7356084-1-9(paper)
ISBN 978-1-7356084-0-2 (ebook)

Printed in the United States of America

Designed by CB Grubb

For Francesca . . .

and all our mothers

Unknown Bodies

out of unknown bodies
we come
slippery from moist spun space
an echo across light years
from the tunneled silence

we come

out of unknown bodies
our own and its opposite
alien as first breath
grappling on the ground of wonder

out of unknown bodies
we become
our own unknown body
crying across
a loop of time

Janine M. Veto 1978

Contents

Don't Ask

As a capgun cowgirl c. 1954, Villa Park, Illinois.

The Dream in a Garden

Until Peter Cappelli, the cop's son, wrested the muddy kickball out of my arms, yelling, "Gimme that, you bastard. Get out of my way," and ran off the field, the tails of his red and black checkered flannel shirt flapping, I had believed that being adopted was special in a *good* way. Now, an opaque scrim flashed inside my skull backlighting a shadowy figure on a previously darkened stage as an inner roar worked through the molten mess of my guts newly flushed with fiery shame. Bastard.

How did he know?

A thin veil over the happy talk about adoption had been torn to reveal a darker truth. No one in my family ever used the word *bastard*, but in that moment in the school yard of Lincoln School in Villa Park, Illinois, 1957, a faint yet fecund figure loomed before me and initiated a haunting: that "other" mother. The *body* that gave birth to me was different from the impeccably dressed, always in earrings and wearing red lipstick, sweet smiling mother I knew. There was no getting around the fact that the nuns had to get me from somewhere before they gave me to the Vetos, but that other body, that unknown body, was somehow connected to a mortal sin that, in turn, created me. I was automatically tainted by the mere fact of being born. A bastard. In my eight-year-old Catholic-trained mind, I wondered whether I would go directly to hell if I died before I could get to confession on Saturday. Could the priest absolve me of this sin with a few rosaries and added devotion to the Blessed Virgin Mary, who, in my mind, had a lot in common with my mother, Marie Walton Veto?

This expulsion from the Garden marked my official loss of innocence and the beginning of my indelible outsider status. My entry into the world was both an unwanted, shameful surprise and a greatly anticipated, celebratory debut. Mine is the jagged story of every child born to a woman in strained circumstance and the anxious adoptive parents awaiting her arrival. Passing between the two camps, a DMZ separates the warring factions where conflicting loyalties lurk.

I retreated from the playground imbued with my terrible new knowledge and forever after heard my origin story in a quite different way.

I had believed that mine was a happy story set squarely in the framework of the realized American Dream. My Viennese mother immigrated to the United States with her parents and moved to a working-class Chicago neighborhood shortly before the Great War. Her father found occasional work as a pants presser in a tailor shop and her mother took in laundry to earn money while she raised five children. Papa Walton was almost deaf due to a blow on the head from his drunken stepfather and, even as a child, I could see how my mother felt protective toward him. To bring in extra money, he raised hundreds of canaries, whose songs he could not hear, in the alcove upstairs next to where my mother slept. She never could bear to be around caged birds after that. One of her greatest pleasures during my childhood was gazing out her kitchen window at birds pecking at the seed she poured into feeders and spread on the lawn.

As the eldest, my mother was the first to attend school and face the horror of hearing a foreign language unable to respond. She learned English quickly and became the one who broke ground so that the family could follow. She quit school after eighth grade and worked so the others could finish high school. And she was the one who remained the chief counsel to her sisters, far into her eighties as they died, one by one, all the younger ones, until only she remained. No wonder she learned to suppress emotion, keep a tight rein on her feelings. As reigning matriarch, she could never let down her guard.

My father's early years were livelier, if not more prosperous. Emil Veto was raised in an Italian neighborhood on the west side of Chicago. He had to transfer streetcars two times to reach my mother's neighborhood during their courting years. My father cited this fact as further proof—as if it were needed—of his singular passion and devotion to my mother. My fantasy about my father's childhood involves a cacophony of Puccini arias, mandolins, and sweaty moral battles over whether recklessly handsome young men with greased-back black hair should join the mob.

Papa's parents immigrated to Chicago from a small town in the mountainous wilds of Calabria and had six sons and a daughter in ten years. The youngest boy and the baby girl died within two weeks of each other during the influenza epidemic that swept the globe in 1918. I have seen their small graves at Mount Carmel Cemetery outside Chicago and the porcelain death pictures set into the headstones; the bodies posed stiffly in fancy dress; the dead eyes already familiar with eternity. My father told me there was a perpetual string of solemn parties for months. The entire neighborhood was in mourning and there was a waiting list at the cemeteries. Burial crews worked around the clock. The shops were emptied of food for the wake parties, and the unstricken children wandered from house to house gorging themselves on the feasts of life that follow Italian death.

My parents, Emil Veto and Marie Walton, 1933, Chicago.

My parents met at the Aragon Ballroom in the late twenties shortly before the stock market crash. A spinning mirrored ball dappled the band and dancers with light. My mother's gold spangled hat caught his eye. He asked her to dance and told her he sold real estate—a whimsical fabrication. He took a photo of a girl from his wallet and claimed it was his girlfriend. "Nice," my twenty-two-year-old mother offered. "She doesn't interest me any longer," he retorted and tore up the photo on the spot to my mother's astonishment. He offered to take her home—the brothers had borrowed a more affluent friend's car. She declined, saying she was going home with one of her sisters. The next Saturday they met and danced again. This time the Veto brothers took the Walton sisters home in a cab. "Don't get used to this," warned my father. "I can't afford it every week. We have to start saving for the wedding."

From the first night he danced with her, my father had made up his mind to marry my mother. Over a period of seven years he wore her down with his off-key mandolin serenades, his off-beat humor, his genuine kindness, and maddening refusal to take no for an answer. My reserved mother had not planned to marry. She was secure in her job as an executive secretary, lived at home and drove a bright red roadster. Who was this funny man with bad skin, two years her junior, who behaved as if he owned her from the moment they met?

My mother and father courted through the Depression and considered themselves fortunate to be employed. They married in 1935 when my mother was twenty-nine and my father twenty-seven. The years passed; hundreds of meat loaf dinners were consumed, photo albums filled with vacation snapshots in the Wisconsin Dells of the two of them with their siblings sporting a succession of styles of the thirties and forties. Baby pictures of nieces and nephews appeared, but there were no photos of children of their own. They consulted doctors, and while nothing tangible could be found, they grew to accept the fact that after ten years of marriage they could not have children. They must have mourned this fact but I never heard about this sorrow from either of them, ever, although I understood my mother's wounding once I was an adult.

My parents were poised to join the parenting stampede of the budding Baby Boom that started in the early 1940s. They were researching adoption options when the ominous long envelope containing the "Greetings" letter from the President, congratulating Mr. Emil Veto on being drafted, landed in their mail box. They were shocked. My father was thirty-five, too old, they had thought, to be called into the war that already had two of his brothers fighting up the boot of Italy and my mother's brother in Britain.

It was then that they forged their dream. My parents tended a Victory Garden fifteen miles west of the city in an area that was rapidly becoming a suburb on the western line of the Chicago-North Western commuter railroad. When he returned from the war, they would purchase the half-acre, build a house, and adopt two children—a boy and a girl—to raise along with the tomatoes, cucumbers, peppers, and strawberries. Were they channeling the lyrics from "Tea for Two," a song popular from their courting days that enjoyed a renaissance in 1950 with the release of the Doris Day film? "A boy for you, a girl for me," warbled Doris.

My parents adopted my brother Bob within the first year of my father's return from the South Pacific. I followed Bob four years later and, when I was two years old, we moved from the apartment in Chicago into our tawny brick ranch-style house financed by a GI loan. It had three bedrooms, a full basement, and low cabinets to accommodate my mother's short reach. After that move in 1951, time stopped. Papa took the 8:04 train into the city, arrived home on the 6:35, and we ate dinner at 6:45. Two-week summer vacations were spent in the Wisconsin North Woods learning to swim and water ski, fish for perch and pick blueberries in the woods. Nothing changed except the steady growth of the Scotch pines, the lilac bushes, Bob, and me.

With my father, brother Bob, and newly planted pine, 1955.

How could I disturb this lovely story with the happy ending for these good, deserving people? I kept my mouth shut when we would gather in the living room to hear "our" story read aloud by mother. *The Chosen Baby*, published in 1939, was a thin volume that resided on a shelf in the latticed-front secretary in the living room along with *Gone with the Wind* (movie version, with full color photos), a joke book bound in red, two novels by Mark Twain, a fishing guide, and *The Poems of Percy Bysshe Shelley*, inscribed to my mother by an admirer in 1924. The Vetos kept "good things" for a long time, which was a very reassuring trait to adopted children.

Bob and I would sit on the green-and-gold-striped couch in our living room next to our mother, our father in his brown corduroy easy chair next to us, and gaze at the pastel drawings as Mama narrated. It is the story about a loving couple who go someplace to look at babies and choose a dark-haired baby boy in fuzzy blue pajamas to bring home. When he is old enough to toddle, a rosy little girl swathed in pink and crowned with a halo of yellow hair is chosen to fill his vacant crib. They are both loved extravagantly by their parents and made to feel more special than children that appear in the usual fashion (never explained) to conventional parents. It was our story, exactly. Bob's life officially began shortly after a nun called the Vetos, telling them it was time to pick up their baby boy. My life officially began four years later when a similar call was placed. If you think about that long enough, it is strange to believe you came from the home of celibate nuns in the first place.

Yet after the shock of Peter's schoolyard cussing, the story frightened me for the very reason that it *was* my story and left so many dark holes filled with mystery. Where would I have gone if my parents did not choose me? Would I have stayed with the nuns? And *who* gave me to the nuns in the first place and *why* did they give me away? I thought that maybe if I heard the story enough times, some new piece of information would be slipped in to give me a clue. My parents were more than happy to reread the book as it evoked happy memories for them. But the story never varied. Longing, fantasy, and an unspeakable fear became braided inside my attentive silences as I came to understand that no other information would be forthcoming.

Not long after my playground trauma, I was walking home after school with my new friend, Ginger Lundstrom. I was old enough to make friends with children who did not live on my block. I told her that I was adopted, still believing it was a positive attribute regardless of what Peter had spouted out a few weeks earlier. By then I had learned that Peter called everyone "bastard" and that he had no idea what it meant or that I was adopted. In fact, that rough, cute bad boy with his ragged brown hair that looked like it had been hacked by a dull Bowie knife, had a crush on me, the one girl who could play baseball as well as he did. I thought adoption was an okay "getting to know you" piece of information for Ginger. Wrong. Her face morphed into a mask of pure horror above the white rabbit collar she wore over her yellow sweater, an ensemble that I secretly envied.

"Oh, oh, I'm so sorry," she cried. "Do you know who your *real* parents are?"

Dumbfounded, I experienced a shock like the one Peter had inflicted on me with his "bastard" remark, but this one put in question the legitimacy of my entire family. Plus, she was crossing that taboo territory about those "other" now fully Zombified parents. Before I could respond, she grabbed my hand and ran me to her house, unable to wait for her mother's take on this bit of exotica. Thankfully, her mother, who was our Brownie troop leader, did not have the same explosive response, although her tone clearly conveyed the notion that I was to be pitied for my condition.

And so, the second prong on the pitchfork that pierced my gut was identified: the parents I loved so dearly were not authentically mine, and those other parents, who were somewhere swimming in sin, were my "real" parents. It was pure luck that I had landed so well. The corollary to this fact, that I understood even then, was that if I was chosen, then I could also be unchosen. Abandonment fears became the piercing final, third prong of the pitchfork, a wound that has never fully healed. I do not remember if Ginger and her mother said how lucky I was not to end up in an orphanage, but if they didn't say it, there were plenty of other people through the years who did.

From these two shocks, delivered hard one upon the other, I became aware of the shame of my existence that could not be erased by any amount of good behavior. Shackled to that was the necessity of being an exceptionally good girl so that I would continue to be chosen and protected from the pit of my sinful beginnings. Or belatedly sent to that orphanage. The woman who carried me for nine months did not want me. From the moment of first breath, I was unwanted. Yes, I was spectacularly lucky to have the Vetos, but even at the age of eight, I knew that luck, like a fat bag of Halloween candy, would one day run out, and that the goblins would come to get me.

By all outward standards I continued to enjoy a secure and happy childhood. It was only within my inner fantasy life that the split, the separateness, the feeling of difference took root and grew through the years; not as a constant, but in flashes and silent moments of recognition. I became aware that I was somehow misplaced, like an exotic night-blooming plant in a merciless, unshaded desert. Beneath the gloss of everyday order dwelt a kingdom of ghosts that had coupled in an unknown past to produce me. I never spoke of them, not even to my brother. To do so would have been an unthinkable betrayal of our parents. But these ghosts lived within me, as many incarnations, through the years.

Sometimes these phantom parents took the form of star-crossed lovers, breathtakingly beautiful and tragic in the impossibility of their love. Other times they moved in darker regions of my psyche; inhabitants of shady, thrilling port towns at the mercy of the cruel forces of the sea. I got a lot of my fantasy material from watching "The Early Show" after school, which offered a rich array of black and white movies from the '30s and '40s, from Barbara Stanwyck noir to the

My Willowbrook High School graduation photo, 1967, one week after my braces came off.

boozy glamour of Nick and Nora Charles in an Art Deco Manhattan. Always, always, my fantasy parents were exceptional and romantic, at the other end of the universe from a brick ranch house in a midwestern suburb in the 1950s where everyone slept in single beds, and none of us ever saw another one naked.

I pursued an exhausting course of perfection and popularity to prove that I was worth being "chosen." I had long blond hair and olive-green eyes; an Alice in Wonderland with bright satin ribbons woven into my hair by my mother; a straight A student; a natural athlete, who read voraciously and dreamed of becoming a writer. The Sunday School nuns showered me with thrilling lace-bordered holy cards that depicted anorexic saints dotted with arrows and bleeding sacred hearts ensnared in barbed wire. My excellent memory also allowed me to memorize the blue-covered Baltimore Catechism, the guide that contained all the beliefs that were required to be a Catholic, and repeat it on demand. Round embroidered merit badges encrusted my green Girl Scout uniform sash. I learned to dance on point, play piano études and ride five-gaited horses. I commanded student councils, edited school newspapers, appeared in the Prom court and won two college scholarships. All through elementary and high school I was much too busy to give any energy or thought to my adoption or to those "other" parents. Without knowledge of heritage, ethnicity or even a medical history, I was busy creating my own identity.

The zombie birth parents slept.

The Graduate

"Sure, take my car," said Tom, his eyes rotating upwards making him appear to be following a ping pong match on a screen embedded in the ceiling. "I have to work on the Duchamp piece this weekend. I wouldn't be much company anyway."

"Thanks," I said lightly, scooping up the Volvo keys on the hook near the front door to his condo. "Maybe if I get away a bit, I can figure out some things." Like my entire post-college life. I knew how to do school, but my next move was unclear.

Tom was one of my boyfriends my senior year at Northwestern. I had started dating him the previous semester when I was in his popular class on the philosophy of art. In those days, sleeping with your professors was not considered sexual harassment nor politically incorrect. I typed his articles for *Art Forum* and he paid for dinners. It was an affair of amiable convenience that was never meant to outlast the school year.

For a long time, I could pretend that my inner chaos was on par with the confusion of my entire generation. I had entered college at the age of eighteen with my virginal wardrobe of matching Villager skirts and sweaters. I pledged a sorority. Within a year I was wearing bell-bottomed jeans and a head band, helped organize a walk-out to protest the mandatory curfew for women in dorms, and was having regular sex with my theatrical bisexual boyfriend. The aftershocks of the Viet Nam War had radically altered the career plans of my Baby Boom generation. Corporate life had become synonymous with the manufacture of napalm, with profits measured by the metric of body counts. I had interned at CBS in Chicago and worked at another television station during the summers, but the idea of toiling in mainstream media had lost its allure. So now what? I didn't know what I would study in graduate school, and besides, classmates with money had rejected that option to hit the road for Canada to escape the draft or to India to seek enlightenment; others like me took jobs as carpenters and waitresses or simply dropped out. I had not gotten to full drop out mode yet, but I know I did not want to waitress the rest of my life. Even the Peace Corp, draped in the glamor and good will of John F. Kennedy's Camelot, was suspect. I opened the envelope that offered me a position in Micronesia to teach English after graduation and quietly put it aside. Who wanted to represent America when the country's policy justified the killing of hundreds of thousands of innocent people?

I drove west out of Chicago through the flat, deadening farmland that marooned the upward stretching city like a lost island. I was wild with the desire to break out of the Midwest, but the only job I had secured so far was working for a YMCA camp in Michigan in July teaching little girls how to shoot .22-caliber rifles. Another one of my boyfriend/professors was making contacts for me with an international peace organization outside New York City, which would at least get me to the east coast, but there was no guarantee that would work out.

In midafternoon I pulled into a small state park in a wooded area. After walking the trails for an hour, I sat down under a white pine by a stream and unwrapped my lunch—processed cheddar cheese, apples, and a bottle of Zinfandel that I had picked up at a country store. I thought this all very European and sophisticated. Ah, if only I could get myself to Europe. I adored French Existentialism, German philosophy, Russian and English nineteenth and twentieth century literature. All that was profound and worthy lay eastward and across the Atlantic.

Using wine as an aid to deep thought was emblematic of the cracks that had developed in the "good girl" façade I had cultivated so carefully through the years. While I missed only four classes in my entire college career, I had also developed a party mode that left me with weekend hangovers and anonymous sex with more guys than I felt comfortable admitting to myself. It was easy to miss the early signs of alcoholism. It was an era when getting high was a sacrament and casual sex the mark of an evolved being. My behavior hardly stood out. I did not learn until I got sober when I was thirty-eight, however, that not everyone blacks out after four drinks.

Warm with wine and the sonorous music of running water, I nodded off. When I woke, the shadows of the pine stretched all the way across the stream to the opposite bank. I gathered up the remains of my lunch and hurried back to the car. I had no idea how far I would have to travel to find a motel in the wide expanse of farmland.

It was almost dark when I passed the pockmarked white sign for a town named Polo and spied a shabby old hotel next to the railroad tracks. The lobby had a musty, time-is-stopped feeling that matched my mood. The desk clerk eyed me suspiciously from behind his rimless glasses, but as I produced both a respectable suitcase and the four-dollar fee up front, he could not refuse me a room. He handed over one of the rusty keys that dangled above the pigeonholed mail sorter behind him and waved me towards the dark staircase.

My room was on the second floor, halfway down a hall smelling of mildew and urine. Once inside, I spread out on the creaky old bed with its battered iron headboard and opened a notebook. What I felt at that moment was something akin to the building of a storm on the prairie when a dark mass on the horizon rolls towards you, gathering speed and height until you are totally enveloped and a slash of lightning like a hot, jagged wire slices open a swollen cloud and the steel-tipped rain shoots down. It had started back at the park when I woke up by the stream. Or perhaps it was earlier, rooted somewhere in a dream whose images were lost but whose energy carried me along to the moment when the poem "Mama One, Mama, Too" gushed from me in one long sob.

Mama One, Mama, Too

I.

Your flecked old hands
quiver threading a needle
Mama, I know
I'll inherit that lace banquet cloth
ringed with cherubs
I never saw you use
along with the painfully precise
family files and photo albums
I saw you fondle
through the years
you called me a "Chosen Child"
and have the papers and memories
to prove it

II.

they say we have similar gestures
you packed my balanced lunch
using six staples and a rubber band
writing my name on three sides
last name, first name, middle initial
period
you packed me in snow suits
puffing me up to a Zeppelin
immobile on my varnished sled
with safety runners
on snowcapped any hills

I bet you wished you could have
packed my knees together, too
Mama, I know
you gave me a sturdy bra
but what about the watermelon breasts
of ladies on playing cards Papa kept
behind the bar and
puffed out bellies of women smiling in public
admitting all ?

III.

they say we are similar through the eyes ...
yours are Alp ice blue
within the waltz city of your nativity
the green of mine does not root
in suburban lawns swamp sources are more likely
or spiral smoke rings from a hookah
floating in illusion
you were proud of the budding scholar
ruining my eyes reading under covers
six years old? what age?
Mama, I was getting fucked over
a thousand times carried down rivers
becoming a mystic
within those womb warm walls

cross-legged on my white colonial bedspread
in the dust-free cubicle
I crawled
through the gutters of port towns
ripped by briny lovers

IV.

they say I have another name …
different from the one on my lunch bags
and the diplomas and awards and certificates
you have tenderly fitted and framed
thank you
for my childhood
I think   thank you   I suppose
for your pragmatic legacy and Lysol halls
I stare at your tidy body
plummeting for some recessed pool than can
Explain my undulations
some hoped for fire
to melt this Golden Girl   from a craven image
back to the crucible
where
I was conceived
back even further
to the forbidden frozen instant
when unsanctioned assent crazed the air

V.

she carried me full nine moons
Mama
from that second
yes
delivering me safely to your stability
with relief, with regret, repulsion
I will never know
how
you sit across the room
mending a cherub, Mama
mindful of thrift

the value of a good name
you smile across
to your tastefully upholstered daughter
whose
swamp eyes shroud:
vision of vacant Alps
packed under a cloud

The dry cough of an old man in the room next door snapped me back to the living moment. It was the quiet, still of the night. Pages ripped from the notebook were scattered around me on the crumpled bedspread. I gathered up the sheets, my hands shaking, and stacked them in a pile in front of me. I uncorked the half bottle of wine leftover from lunch, took a long swallow and started to read.

When I finished, I dropped the pages, my teeth clenched. Anger? Was the scream inside me anger? I was petrified. Somehow getting angry about my birth was as forbidden as wanting to know how a woman of flesh and passions poured herself into my very being and then disappeared. What I had just written trashed my neat narrative of a happy childhood and uncovered a taboo anger directed at my mother. A deep place in me howled for the woman I lost at birth; the one who had sex and passion and, lest I forget, *shame* for having given me birth. I was part of that outcast body, and I had no way to reach out and touch her. And I did, indeed, want to touch her. The poem was a call to action, but I was not ready to respond. I just needed to get out, to get moving. To run away.

***

It was not until four years later that I stopped running. And even then, it was not by choice.

After graduation I drifted between New York, San Francisco, and Honolulu; between jobs in television and public relations; between a series of lovers, male and female, younger and older and of at least three races. I told myself I liked adventure and change. I thought I was accumulating experience for books I would write at some future date. After four years of this, I found myself engaged to a German sea captain. It was planned that I would join him in Hamburg after a quick visit with my parents and friends in the Midwest. Once in Chicago, I placed several expensive overseas calls to let Jens know when to expect me, but he never answered. Then I wrote letters which seemed to drop into a void. Finally, I got in touch with his friend and shipmate, who politely replied that he never got involved in Jens' business. That was my last communication from Germany.

I was stunned. Stunned and humiliated. But the fact was that I was not all that in love with Jens in the first place; he was part of the romance of the life I was leading at the time. I had also been having an affair with a woman in Honolulu, for whom I had much deeper feelings than I had for Jens. She had two young sons from her former marriage and a current boyfriend. Neither one of us was at the stage where we could imagine that a primary relationship could be forged with another woman.

In any case, after a month moping around in my parents' home, where I thought I had just stopped for a visit, I "got it" that I was in Chicago to stay. My parents did not press me about plans, but I could not hang out in my old bedroom forever. I also felt a self-imposed pressure to look like I was okay to them even when I felt everything but okay about my sexuality, my career prospects, or my ability to have just one or two drinks once I started. I rented a room in a married college friend's big old house in nearby Evanston and started to hunt for a job. I still looked good on paper and my inquiries brought several responses. I frequented hangouts both gay and straight which often led to black-out sex with people I would have had no interest in when sober.

One spring morning when I had an interview scheduled with a Chicago public relations firm, I instead lay whimpering under the bedcovers, unable to get up. I studied the movement of leaf patterns on the ceiling from the dormer window, my mind as blank as a whiteout. A rented room. In Evanston near the campus I had left four years earlier in 1971. How did I boomerang back here?

Ha! I could not even get up to go to the bathroom although my bladder was about to burst. I could not imagine how I would make it through a job interview. The last time I was stopped still in my tracks a poem sounded the alarm bells to my brain. This time, in one of those improbable moments of grace, the phone rang on my bedside table. I somehow, in slow motion, drew my arm up and over the covers to pick up the receiver. A friend, who just happened to be a therapist, heard my voice, and knew instantly that I was in crisis. Those who knew me as the high achieving, pleasant co-ed did not know that I silently suffered through these punishing mornings on an increasing basis.

Within twenty-four hours she had me hooked up with another therapist who, over a period of months, helped me to see that I was, indeed, in crisis and that accepting that state as the new normal was not a healthy choice. In the process of rooting out the problem, I was also learning just why abandonment would forever be a wound at the very core of my being. I was twenty-five and it was time to face the fears that had erupted in that fleabag hotel room four years earlier. I had been looking for myself in seascapes, paychecks and embraces rather than facing the fact that I lived in a world cleaved in half: I was the accomplished daughter of loving parents; I was the bastard offspring of outlaw lovers who gave me away. And that bothered me. Deeply. Gradually I could acknowledge that I really did want to know who these other parents were, for better or worse. I needed reality more than shiny (or scary) fantasies. Action was required. I needed to go on a quest. Somewhere here in the city where I was born lay the threads that could lead me back through the fictions of my birth, back to the woman who bore me so that I could unravel the mystery of my ancestry and learn why I was given away.

But where to start?

The answer did not emerge right away. But now emotionally stronger and focused, I was able to move out of my friend's attic into my own place in Chicago. I got a job as a Continuity Director at a public television station. The basic requirements had fallen into place, although the path to finding my birth parents was still not clear.

I was sitting on the couch in my new sparsely furnished apartment in Rogers Park on the tenth floor overlooking Lake Michigan. This was eight months after moving out of the attic. The rent was more than I could afford on my salary, but it was worth the sacrifice of other pleasures like going to the movies and eating out. I did allow myself the luxury of buying both the *New York Times* and the *Chicago Tribune* for my Sunday reading fest, however. I would read a section, refill my coffee cup, look at the progression of light on the still lake, then return to the paper. A headline in the feature section of the *Tribune* caught my eye: "Yesterday's Children Have Far to Go – To Find Identity Through Courts."

The story detailed the filing of a test case to have adoption files opened to adoptees over the age of twenty-one who wanted their birth information. A local group, calling itself Yesterday's Children, had brought the class action suit on behalf of adoptees who wanted access to their own birth information. At the end of the article was information about the group and the date of their next meeting, only two days away in nearby Evanston. I immediately knew I needed to be there. As the time for the meeting drew near however, my euphoria gave way to an acute attack of anxiety. I arrived at the Evanston library fifteen minutes early and sat in the car smoking cigarettes for half an hour before I got up enough nerve to enter the building. I finally made myself climb the stairs to the meeting room and dove into a seat at the back. I do not know what I had expected, but what I found was a decidedly average looking group of people. I thought they would have a more clandestine air or sinister sheen. I could not get over the notion that in trying to find my birth parents I was doing something criminal.

That first night I sat in my folding chair at the back, clutching my coffee and glazed doughnut, and listened to a genial, elderly genealogist explain ethnic migration patterns in the Midwest. Some people nodded and scribbled notes in fat notebooks brimming with scraps and clues. Others gazed off as if this were territory they had already exhausted, or perhaps couldn't start to explore because they didn't even know their ethnicity.

After the lecture, a half dozen men and women stood up to deliver reports about the end of their searches—a married sister found in Minneapolis, a father traced to a grave in Florida, a mother located in the next suburb but not yet contacted. A palpable charge coursed through the room. This was the real heart of the meeting. The search stories were bulletins from the front. These people had found connections to those who shared their blood. It did not seem to matter *what* or *whom* they found; the connection itself was the focus of their passion.

The group then broke up into small workshops to share techniques and strategies for The Search. I turned my chair to join the cluster of women nearest me.

Most of the members of Yesterday's Children were female, which was typical, I was to learn. It was easy for me to understand this from the viewpoint that women bear children and are intimately concerned about how their unknown genes would impact their child. Studies show that girls often become curious about their birth mothers when they themselves reach the same age as their unknown birth mother and can well imagine how they might feel themselves if pregnant.

I began filling the pages of my new spiral notebook with ways on how to close the net around a phantom parent by tracking down city directories, old phone books, agencies, military records, motor vehicle licenses, marriage and death certificates and cemetery records. It was a crash course in sleuthing. My mind flipped to the memory of the long row of blue cloth-bound volumes of Nancy Drew mysteries I had devoured as a girl. From fairy tales of changelings to "adult" stories of mistaken identity, I possessed a lifelong fascination for this sort of story line. I was in the right place.

The information was invaluable, but as I looked at my notes, I realized that I had no point of departure for my own search. Suddenly my chest ached as I struggled to hold back tears. I simply did not know my name. Oh, I had a *name* and an altered birth certificate to prove I was "legitimate." It was a lie, of course. My original name was sealed away by court order along with my original birth certificate and the names of those other parents. It was considered a kindness in those days to protect a child from bastard status.

"Okay, all of you without a name, come here." I turned toward the voice of Sandra Mullen, the president of the group, who was gathering a cluster of people around her. "How many of you were born in Chicago?" she demanded. "Write your given name and birth date on this paper. And your daytime phone number. I am making a trip to the *Law Bulletin* next week. I'll get your real names."

"How can you do that?" It was the first time I had spoken the entire evening.

Sandra Mullen flashed a triumphant smile. She stood with a hand on one hip and her abundant red hair tossed over a shoulder, a tableau of a fighting Irish lass.

"Easy. Adoption is a legal proceeding, isn't it? So, a legal notice must be published. In Illinois, adoptions are valid six months after the placement of a child. All I need to do is look at the old microfilm of the *Chicago Daily Law Bulletin*. It usually shows up seven to ten months after your birth. A docket number can confirm it. Or the date of your 'corrected' birth certificate helps pinpoint the time. If you were born in Chicago, you're in luck. And the *Bulletin* hasn't caught on to what we're doing yet."

I scribbled the information from my birth certificate down on her sheet. It seemed impossible that it should be so easy. And to compound the coincidence, my Uncle Bill had been a reporter with the *Bulletin*. I had even worked in his office as a proofreader one summer during high school, seated next to the very room that held the microfilm Sandra Mullen would scan to find my name.

I was jumpy and excited for days. I made errors on the timing of promos and newsbreaks between programs and had to redo entire air logs once I discovered my mistakes. I was having difficulty keeping my mind focused on details. Yet I dared not tell anyone at work why I was distracted. In the competitive television world, weaknesses were exploited. I did not talk about adoption, and I did not talk about the woman I was living with. Silence on these topics and job security went hand in hand in the 1970s. I shared my office at the station with my assistant and two air directors, so I was fortunate to be alone in the office the afternoon I picked up my phone and a woman's voice asked, "Alana Phipps, is that you?"

"No, what department did you want?" I responded, annoyed.

"Oh, I think I have the right department, Janine. This is Sandra Mullen coming to you straight from a phone booth outside the *Chicago Daily Law Bulletin*. I got your name, honey. It's Alana Phipps. No doubt about it. Your parents' names are on the notice. The dates check. It's you. Alana Phipps. How do you like it?"

How did I like it? That was like asking a child who has hankered for a dog her whole life what breed she prefers. Kids just want a dog they can call their own. Breed and purity of lineage is an adult preoccupation. Alana Phipps sounded exotic, mysterious, and magical. I had a name. Sandra Mullen, a stranger, had given me the one thing no one had been able to give me my entire life—my name; what I was first called out of the womb.

At that heady, triumphant moment it was good that I did not know what lay in front of me. How was I to know that to find out who I was I would have to face down the guardians of The Church? The State? That I would have to crush family harmony? That I would have to assert my rights and quell my deepest fears to find out my lineage, my heritage, my own mother?

Subversion

The Catholics

I stood outside Catholic Charities' sprawling headquarters on a nippy autumn morning with my hands jammed into the pockets of my "good" coat and pushed down the nausea that threatened to erupt into a Vesuvian display of projectile vomiting against the massive front door. Having a hangover did not add to my composure as I approached that Citadel of the Faithful that occupied an entire block of Des Plaines Avenue on Chicago's west side. I would not be here if I could find any other way to find information about my birth mother.

A quarter of a century earlier, in this very building, papers were signed that changed my name and life forever. By law, I had no right to know more. To gain access to any of that information, I would once again have to become the good little girl, anxious to please. I was full of rage, but I knew I had to keep a cool head. I hadn't had a dress on in almost two years, but for the occasion I had put together an outfit of tasteful camel-colored skirt and sweater, accented with a gold cross necklace I had purchased at the Ben Franklin store in my neighborhood. Freshly washed hair and a light application of lipstick completed the costume. I was as ready as I ever was going to be.

The euphoria of securing my original name had propelled me throughout the summer. I picked up techniques and clues for hunting down my quarry from Yesterday's Children and stuffed my burgeoning search file with notes along with pages ripped from phone books, columns of "Phipps" neatly marked through with black ink. After six months of frenzied effort, however, most of my prospects had been eliminated. Not one Phipps family I had phoned seemed to be related to me, but I could not be sure. I simply did not have enough information to enable me to narrow the field. How old was my mother when she gave birth to me? Where was she from? Was Phipps even her real name? Or if it were, wouldn't she be married now, with a different name? There were too many key facts missing.

Just when my despair was cresting, hope was rekindled in September. Several of my fellow adoptees had gone back to the agencies from which they had been adopted and had simply asked for their records. The real surprise was that many of them came away with useful information. I immediately planned a sick day from the office and looked up the address of Catholic Charities.

Catholic authority was the guardian of the first gate to the secret chamber of my beginnings. I was seething with resentment at a church that, to my mind, was a hypocritical power broker staffed by an arrogant and privileged male hierarchy. This intellectualized attitude, fed by the then newly minted feminist rhetoric, had evolved in me over the years. Once upon a time, I had been enchanted with Catholic myth and ritual and the certainties of fish on Friday and a white lace dress at First Communion. I was proud of my membership in the One True Faith, even though my best friend was a Lutheran and was, *ipso facto,* going to hell. This specialness fit in with my other special status as an adopted child. But as I grew in sophistication and awareness, I realized that no matter how many times the nuns rewarded me with holy cards, I was never going to be allowed to serve at the alter during Mass. Quiet rage was ignited with the knowledge that my beloved Church would love me back only in proportion to my subjugation and acceptance as a second-class being. This is a particularly painful position to be in if your beloved is also your spiritual home and avenue for your own transcendence. Besides, Catholicism was simply too narrow a lens through which to view the world during my expansive intellectual and sexual development at the dawning of the Age of Aquarius. Solace and certainty were for the infantile, I declared with all the vigor and health of youth. The Catholic Church had duped me, and I had righteously exited its domain in my teens. Now the church had something I needed, and the old position of suppliant was the only way I was going to get it.

"Damn them," I hissed under my breath as I swung open the door into the lobby. "The Catholics always want you on your knees."

The entrance hall of the building was drafty, dimly lit and suffused with a dank, musty odor. To my right, an elderly woman operated an old-fashioned switchboard. Behind the pane of glass supported by a scarred wood frame, she stared blankly at her console as if in a trance. When a red light flashed, she blinked imperceptibly, drew out a long tentacle of wire and plugged it in beneath the light. Was she in the throes of the Beatific Vision, lobotomized, or merely harnessed to this job for so long that conscious thought was neither required nor desired? I wondered if her younger self had sat just so twenty-five years before when my pregnant mother crossed this very threshold.

I approached the reception desk situated at the corner of the glassed-in area and waited until she finished scribbling and finally glanced up.

"I'd like to see a social worker, please," I smiled pleasantly and hoped she took note of the cross at my throat.

"Do you have an appointment?" She inspected me with a vertical scan of her eyes.

"No, but isn't one free?"

"Well, you should really make an appointment," the woman sniffed. "What is this regarding?"

"Please. Could you just see if someone is free? It's about an adoption. Mine." I let out a long, slow breath to calm my suddenly accelerated heartbeat.

"Very well. Wait over there." She sniffed again as she rose from her desk and disappeared through the door behind the reception area.

I perched on the edge of a chair and fumbled for a cigarette. The whole room was frozen in time. The architecture was faded Art Deco. A mismatched assortment of chairs was grouped facing the reception area and the inevitable crucifix.

I turned at the sound of a door opening behind me. The receptionist emerged followed by a thin, grey-haired woman dressed in a gray wool suit, which struck me as a secular compromise between the black and white habits of nuns. As she approached me with short, clipped steps, I stood up to greet her.

"May I help you?" Dull brown eyes studied me from behind steel rimmed glasses.

"Yes. My name is Janine Veto. You see, I was adopted from here and I was wondering what information you could share with me."

The woman blinked, revealing eyelids veined with tiny blue lines. "I see. I am Miss MacFarland. Would you care to step into my office?" I followed her into a tiny cubicle just large enough for an old blond wood desk and two chairs. Miss MacFarland situated herself squarely behind the desk and folded her hands.

"I must prepare you for the fact that the records are not complete. Files have been moved, damaged, and lost over the years. There is no guarantee your file still exists. Nor are we under any legal obligation to share it with you should it exist."

"I understand, Miss MacFarland. I certainly would be grateful for anything you might be able to tell me. I appreciate the delicate position this puts you in."

"I'm glad you understand." She nodded her approval at my answer. "Now, I need your birth date, parents' names, and date of adoption to check."

She took a long look at me, appraising me as if I were a suspected zircon on a tray of diamonds.

"Now, Miss Veto, do you know what hospital you were born in?"

"Yes, Misericordia. In 1949."

We both knew Misericordia Hospital was the Catholic baby factory of the Baby Boom generation. I had tried, unsuccessfully, to obtain my records from it directly two months earlier and learned that it had been converted into a mental institution. The irony did not escape me.

"I see."

I reached into my purse and drew out the document she needed. "Here's a copy of my birth certificate."

Miss MacFarland scanned the photostat and gave a quick nod.

"Yes. This will do. Please stay here while I have them check the records."

My rigid spine gave way as the door clicked behind Miss MacFarland. The urge for a cigarette was overwhelming, but I could not risk the slightest tarnishing of my image. This was a performance and I had to keep in character. I looked around the bare, clean room with a crucifix hanging above the desk chair. A bloody interrogation chamber with the authority of God Almighty backing up the decisions made from that chair, I fumed crazily to myself. A silent rage at my powerless position swept through me.

The door opened with a jerk as Miss MacFarland entered with a manila folder grasped in one hand. She opened the folder and turned the pages slowly. I squirmed in my chair. My file. Everything I needed to know held eighteen inches away at a well-protected angle from my eyes. After turning the last page, Miss MacFarland cleared her throat, closed the file, folded her hands squarely on top of it, and stared straight into my eyes.

"You realize, of course, that I can give you no identifying information. No names, places. That should not make a great deal of difference. Unless, of course, you plan to look for these people."

I immediately sensed the trap and feigned a look of outraged innocence. "Look for them? Why I never even considered that! My mother and father are the finest parents anyone could ask for. Why should I want another set of parents? I just would like to know a little more about my background."

A glob of bile rose in my throat. I was spewing forth the proper, well-adjusted adoptee answer. The myth peddled at that time was grounded in the assumption that a successful adoption was one in which the child had no desire to find the natural parents. A good adoptee was one who possessed no curiosity, was immune to any functions of the body below the neck, and believed her life started at the adoptive home. Questioning was betrayal and a sure sign of neurosis.

"You've had a happy life, then, Miss Veto?"

Oh, I drink too much, sleep with people whose names I do not remember, change jobs and cities every few turns of the seasons, but what is a happy life, Miss Mac? Yours?

From the perspective of several decades later, I can say that the woman was merely performing her professional duties and was very decent to me, a surprise visitor, nudging around an area with ill-defined policy guidelines during an era of transition. But at the time, in the grip of my obsessive need and impatient youth, I harbored hostility towards her as an agent or at least dupe of the enemy forces.

"Oh, yes. I have no argument with my parents. We are very close. In fact, it would have been a crime if they never had had children."

"I'm glad to hear that. According to these files they are a lovely couple. If they had wanted, we would have given them six children."

Instead of receiving the compliment graciously, I felt a surge of hate towards Miss MacFarland. I hated having to trade on my genuine love for my parents to leverage information about those other parents.

"Did you go to college, Miss Veto?"

"Yes, Northwestern. On scholarship."

"That's good." The information pleased her. She made a note in the file. "And what do you do now?"

"I work for the public television station. Continuity Director." What I do not have in my life, I mock with the title of my job, I chatted to myself.

"Not married?"

"No." If she knew that I slept with a woman and a man in a confused rotation of attraction, she would flip the file closed faster than a Three-card Monte dealer.

"It's difficult when one has a career, isn't it?" This confidential aside to me was a good sign. She was warming up. It was maddening to know she could share or withhold information totally on whim. For one crazed moment, I considered grabbing the file from under her firmly folded parchment hands and dashing like a running back for the front door. But I knew I had to continue to be a good girl to fit into Miss MacFarland's notion of propriety. My only route to the truth was through lying to the gate keepers.

"Well, I suppose you'd like to hear a few things. We must be careful, you know. For some reason, we are getting a lot of adoptees returning lately. Some have even formed a group and are rather rude about their demands."

"A group?"

"Yes, they call themselves Yesterday's Children. A rather harsh group, I might add."

"Never heard of them." I felt my eye lashes flutter with the lie.

"They just *demand* their records." Miss MacFarland leaned over the desk toward me. "They have no sensitivity to the delicacy of the situation. I dare say some of them are leading miserable lives and are looking for an excuse to blame someone else. They actually want to find their birth parents. I guess to accuse them or else they have some fairy tale idea that everything would be all right in their lives if they found them. Very immature and not very well adjusted."

"I see. I can understand your difficult position." I swallowed hard and tried to keep my leg from bouncing. I also reminded myself I was wearing a skirt and to keep leg crossing restricted to the ankle area.

"Yes. I thought you would. You seem to be a happy, well-adjusted person. Well, let us see what it says here." She reopened the file, adjusted her glasses, and licked her cracked lips that cried out for Vaseline.

"May I take notes?"

"I suppose so."

"Thank you." I flipped the cover of the spiral steno pad and tried to appear casual. The file was open!

"Now, let's see. You were six pounds, thirteen ounces when you were born and measured fifty centimeters. The labor was an easy one and lasted three hours and twenty minutes. The Vetos took you home on May 30th when you were seventeen days old and weighed seven pounds and seven and a half ounces."

This was the most shocking information I had ever heard about myself. I was *born*. I had a specific physical weightiness. It took three hours to expel me out of the womb of a woman who did not want me. And yet I hung around with her for three weeks before she disappeared into her own life. Was there tenderness between us? Repulsion on her part? Anguish? A surprising gush of love? All the possibilities cartwheeled through my brain. And my reaction? I had images of reaching towards her, turning my head towards her breast, seeking nourishment, comfort, and protection—a continuity, perhaps, from the nine months I grew inside of her to the new air-breathing world she commanded. How much was she able or willing to give me then? Or now?

Fifteen years later I was sitting in a movie theater in Manhattan with two other adopted women. *Immediate Family* was one of the rare films about adoption, and this one had the added spin of depicting an "open adoption" where a teenage mother gets to pick the middle-aged prospective parents to journey together through her pregnancy. During the delivery room scene, the adoptive parents, clad in surgical gowns, flank the teenaged birth mother as the baby emerges from the womb. I stiffened in my seat and felt the same rigid attention in the two women on either side of me. Our three heads exploded like kernels of corn on hot oil. As the credits rolled, we stood up, still silent, and filed out of the theater.

"Goddamn," mumbled Rosemary, "I can't afford to go back to therapy right now. But, God." She shook her head. Ann and I looked at her and nodded, still unable to speak. When we were born, birth and adoptive parents would never have inhabited the same room, let alone share the experience of the birthing of their common child. I had spent years creating that connecting bridge between two mothers and the film still shocked me. Rosemary was actively searching and Ann was considering it. Adoption would never be a fact about ourselves that did not reach deep inside our very being, whether we found that other mother or not.

I scribbled down each scrap of information Miss MacFarland offered with my heart pounding loudly in my ears. I did not have time to absorb the impact of all this momentous information as she droned on. To be physically born of someone meant that the fleshy heritage of that person was embedded in my own body. Birth is what made people look like each other, to have traits in common, good and bad. It is difficult to impress upon most people how startling it is to finally connect to the fact that your flesh is kin with other flesh, living and dead, and that you are not, after all, a disconnected space module floating, untethered in a weightless universe.

"Your mother was nineteen when you were born. She had graduated high school and took a summer office job before her planned entrance into college. She was of French and English descent. Her health was very good. She was attractive and made a good impression. Her skin was clear, she kept herself neat, had even teeth and dimples."

At this bit of news, I let out an involuntary sob. Dimples. The stranger who looked like me.

"Ah, could you stop for a moment, please?" I took off my tear-spotted glasses and reached into my purse for a Kleenex. I worked on controlling the lump in my throat as I methodically polished away the spots. "Thank you for stopping. I just never heard someone who looks like me described before. You can go on now."

"Very well. Let's see. Oh, yes, dimples. She was five feet and five and a half inches tall, weighed about 120 pounds. Brown hair, blue eyes. She was interested in music and Russian literature, perhaps as subjects to take up in college. She did a great deal of reading when she was here. She was from out of town, from a large Midwestern city. She was living with a married sister in an upper middle-class suburb. Your father was twenty-three. He lived in the suburbs and had some college experience. He is Italian." Here Miss MacFarland allowed herself a sniff as she turned the page. "Your mother didn't tell him she was pregnant. She knew in December and entered the maternity home in January, where she stayed until your birth in May. Your mother had a sister who was four years older than she. Also, two older brothers, one married. Two younger brothers and one sister. One of her brothers was an officer in the Army. Your mother said she wanted to marry your father but decided against it and never told him of her pregnancy."

The last bit did not gel. Who would want to marry a guy you could not even tell you were pregnant?

"Her sister and husband offered to raise the child—that's you—jointly with her, but they decided the best thing for the child would be to be raised in an adoptive home." Miss MacFarland's finger rested at the bottom of the page. "Oh, and she didn't legally surrender you until she was up on her feet after the birth. Quite unusual. That's about it."

I kept my head down as if I was checking over my notes. Surrender. The word had the connotation of giving up, of weariness and an all too muchness. After recovering from the birth (I was born!) and on her feet, she gave up on me and walked out of that hospital into her own life, solo. Her decision. Hers alone.

My hand had been shaking so much that the script looked like the journal entries I would make when I was drunk. My brain raced over the details, searching for more questions I could ask, more information I could wrest from my file.

"You say she was living in a northern suburb?"

"No, I didn't say northern. I said upper middle class." The tone was schoolmarmish.

"Oh, I see. The same one my father was from, I suppose?"

"I didn't say that." Now she was slightly irritated. I sensed I should stop. If I pressed any further, my real motive would be apparent. I smiled inwardly. With the Phipps name, ages, and family configuration, I might have enough information to advance my quest in the network set up through my search group.

"Miss Veto, I assume your parents are still alive?"

"Yes, they are." I was caught off guard by the question. I had not anticipated she would want her turn.

"Well, you know we have an association of adoptive parents. In fact, we have a dance coming up. Do you think they'd be interested?"

"Ah, I don't think so, Miss MacFarland. They're out of town now. They're retired and spend the summers at their home in northern Wisconsin. They won't be back for quite a while yet."

"Well, since I have your address, I'll just send you notice of the next social event."

I was incredulous. My parents did not even know I was searching for my birth mother. And as for dances! My parents never even went to PTA meetings when I was a child. Why would they go to an adoptive parents group twenty-five years after the last adoption?

"Sure, just send along the notice. Thank you very much," I vamped.

"You're welcome, dear. I'm glad everything has worked out so well for you."

"Oh, yes. Thank you. Good-bye."

I jumped to my feet, shook Miss MacFarland's hand, and raced out of the room. Once outside, I slumped against a building to catch my breath. With physical details and snatches of history, the reality of my mother as a living human being struck me full force. I needed a drink. I also needed to talk to my parents. I could not keep the search a secret any longer. And Lord knows I had to beat Miss MacFarland's invitation to the dance.

The Family

On the day following my traumatic meeting at Catholic Charities I flew up to the rural Rhinelander, Wisconsin, airport near my parent's summer house to confess (because at that time it felt I was committing a sin) my need to find that other mother and to ask for my mother's help. I was in a state of panic, afraid and yet compelled to find out more. If I felt that confronting The Church was scary, it was nothing compared to my fear of hurting the people I loved most in the world. I was buoyed, however, by the knowledge that my parents had never withheld their love for me. I counted on that.

I waited to broach the subject until my father had taken his boat over to the other side of the lake in his never-ending quest for fish who could be enticed to nibble on his proffered worms or silver spinners. I knew that my mother would tell my father what he needed to know at the right time in the proper dosage. All vital information was filtered through my mother first. I remember my therapist commenting once, "Ah, so you grew up in a matriarchy with two mothers." No wonder I cannot take male posturing and assumption of authority seriously.

Mama was in the kitchen, methodically pounding the raw meat thin enough for Wiener Schnitzel. It reminded me of how she would squeeze all the juice out of cucumbers to make a vinegar salad by covering the slices with waxed paper and slamming down an old flat iron she took with her from her own mother's house. This squeezing and pounding were the only hints of violence I ever witnessed in my home growing up. I sat at the other end of the white Formica kitchen table to wait for the water to boil for my coffee. As the sun caught the gold flecks in the table I squinted and looked up at the calendar towel that hung next to the cuckoo clock. A man leaning on a shovel in a forest. The motto read "He Who Plants Trees Loves Others." On the other side of the clock hung a ceramic Madonna of the Kitchen. The loving virgin wearing a star-spattered pink apron over her snow-white robes rests her hand on the blond head of a little girl who reaches out her hand for the nourishing loaf of bread offered by her mother. Could the iconography be any plainer? I was stalling.

Two hummingbirds zipped past the window. One paused to drink the sweet, red liquid from one of the suspended feeders by thrusting its long needle-like beak into the narrow aperture. The water bubbled in the aluminum saucepan. I got up to pour it over the instant coffee crystals, lit a cigarette as I sat down, and forced myself to speak.

"Mama, I don't know how to start. My biggest fear is that you'll take this the wrong way. But I can't keep it to myself any longer. It would be dishonest."

"Go on, honey." She laid down the mallet and eased into the chair next to me.

"Mama, you've got to understand that I love you very much and it's not because I'm dissatisfied with you and Papa in any way. But in the past few years I've gotten very curious about my adoption and what the story was behind my birth, I mean *before* the nuns and all that, and I couldn't keep it out of my mind."

Once started, I rattled on quickly to bring her up to date on my search, never quite looking her directly in the eye.

"So, when I learned you could find out more information at Catholic Charities, well, I was there yesterday. Oh, and first off, they positively *glowed* about you and Papa and would have given you six kids if you had wanted them. But, anyway, it just totally devastated me, and I had this great need to talk to you and to tell you what I was doing." I stopped short and looked squarely at my mother for the first time.

"I imagined that it might have something to do with the adoption," she said with a slight nod.

"What? How could you know that?"

"When I heard your voice on the phone last night, I thought you could be upset about two or three things that I've been concerned about. And that was one of them."

The other "things," I surmised, were my drinking and my recent defection to Lesbos. I must say, that for turn of the century immigrants, my parents rolled well with a lot of punches. I will be forever grateful for the way they handled my transition to female lovers. Mother had to notice that I was no longer bringing home that sexy bisexual actor who had relieved me of my virginity my freshman year at college, or even the manly German sea captain to whom I had been engaged in Honolulu. But she waited until I brought up the topic before venturing her own opinion. "Oh, my dear, it will be hard for you, I'm afraid," she had said then. Papa had burst into tears at the news and could not talk to me for six months without dissolving in sobs, but then some internal device clicked over in him and it became a non-issue. I brought lovers up to vacation with them over the years, and I appeared at their fiftieth wedding anniversary with the woman I was living with at the time.

"What did you learn at Catholic Charities, honey?" she asked calmly. She nudged a saucer towards me for my cigarette. "Are they still on the west side?"

I filled her in on the information I had gotten from Miss MacFarland the day before. I kept peppering the account with asides about my happy childhood to reassure both of us that my needs would not threaten our bond. But despite my care, I did hurt her. I saw her wince when I told her the nationality of that other mother, French and English.

"Not German?"

"No, Mama. Just French and English as far as I know."

"I thought they told me German."

Ah, there it was. Despite her eight dozen readings of *The Chosen Baby,* it was important to her, this physical heritage likeness between mother and child. I should have fibbed. It was important to my mother, this mirroring of herself in her child. Within the adoption triad, as it came to be called, everyone is traumatized yet what is celebrated is the joy of placing a child in a better situation. This may be true, but to deny that everyone is suffering their own grief is an illusion that shadows the very joy that is promoted so cheerfully.

"Is there anything I can do to help?" she asked.

I did not answer immediately. Almost seventy years old and she was as stalwart as ever. Always there for me, yet never offering a clue to her own carefully guarded feelings.

"I'm secure, darling," she continued. "I know I am your mother and you are truly my daughter. If I were you, I'd probably be curious, too."

"Oh, Mama," I reached across the table and held my mother's hand. "There is one thing that might help. Do you still have the adoption decree? She would have had to sign it to release me."

"Oh, no. I threw those out about five years ago when we went through all our papers with a lawyer. He said we didn't need them any longer. Besides, I don't recall any signature on them. But, yes, the name was Alana for you."

What? She knew my original name and never told me? And then it hit me. As a little girl, I had named my dolls Lana and Alice, although those names were not in our family or in families of children I knew at school. I was called Alana the first three weeks of my life. Could I really have retained a memory of that sound? Did that ever occur to my mother when she heard me play with my dolls? And what else could I remember? The idea that children in their mothers' wombs absorbed their mothers' moods and traumas was just gaining traction.

"The lawyers were Flynn and O'Reilly, if that would help," she continued. "They were very prominent at the time. I don't know if they're still in practice."

"Thanks. I'll remember that. Who knows what will turn the trick? It's such a maze, such a puzzle."

"Just one thing." My mother's jaw clenched.

"Anything." I would have grabbed the meat hammer and dashed my brains out for her at that moment if she had asked.

"If you ever find her, I don't want to meet her. Ever." Her eyes were frozen pools of blue, her face a perfect blank.

"No, of course not. I wouldn't dream of it." It was the only time I saw my mother afraid, and it shocked me.

"Good. I'd have nothing to say to her. You are *my* daughter. She had nothing to do with you. Giving birth does not make someone a mother."

It broke my heart to know that I was the one to press a wound that she concealed so well.

"I know. I know. I'm not looking for another mother." I rushed to console her. So, this was her deeply rooted fear. The natural maternity that was denied to her made my mother vulnerable to an unknown woman who could lay claim to me through the ancient tyranny of blood and birth. I *knew* I had wonderful parents, but I also needed a connection to the intellect, the artsy, the sexy—all those attributes that seemed so urgently important to me in my twenties and for which I could find no trace in my upbringing. Surely, some of these things in me came from those other parents.

I have a brother and two cousins who also were adopted, yet none of them ever expressed the slightest interest in finding their birth families. The one thing I did notice, however, is how young they all were when they started having children—teenagers, for the most part—as if their hunger for familiar flesh and echoed likenesses could only be satisfied by duplication, to get that stranger who looked like them out of their bodies so that they could look at them, touch them, and gather them into their new family circle.

"I have to get back to pounding the veal. They never cut the chops thin enough out here for schnitzel."

"Thanks, Mama. Thank you for everything."

"I love you, Janine. I'd do anything to make you happy."

"And I love you. Please, please never doubt it."

My mother's chapped hand brushed my cheek as she walked past me to the cutting board. I lit another cigarette and gazed dumbly at the hummingbirds and the line of pines leading to the water. Papa had dug them out of the woods as seedlings when my parents had first bought the house after his retirement. They now formed a dark green, feathered wall along the property line. The resumed pounding made my delicate hungover head throb. I got up from the table and made my way across the lawn and down to the redwood deck jutting out into the lake. I sat on the bench at the end under the American flag whipping around the flagpole and let the pressure building in my chest escape into gulping sobs.

I jerked up my head at a buzzing sound from across the lake. My father's aluminum fishing boat had rounded the point and was pointed back towards the dock. I wiped away the tears running down my cheeks so that he would not become upset. As he drew closer, Papa reached down to the bottom of the boat and held up a stringer with two large walleyes and a Northern pike for me to admire. I clapped my hands and forced a smile.

"Nice!" I called out.

Papa jiggled the fish one more time then laid them down. He cut off the motor and glided up to the dock in the suddenly silent afternoon.

"Want to troll a little before dinner?" he asked.

I looked back towards the house. I was not ready to go back yet. I nodded and climbed into the bow and shoved off. Papa moved into the middle seat and set the oars into the locks. We drifted in our comfortable silence for nearly an hour exchanging a few words about bait and the weather. The only other sound was the mournful wail of loon rolling over the water between deep dives to the bottom of the spring-fed lake.

I did not bring up the reason for my sudden visit, nor did he ask. He would learn what he needed to know from my mother. We were still more than a decade away from the manifestation of dementia that would rob my mother of so much of her power.

The State

The initial euphoria over learning my name and piecing together my birth mother's background dwindled over the next several months. I typed out a script for myself and laid it on top of the file of Phipps listings from area phone books that I kept on my desk at home for whenever I built up the courage to make a call. Sometimes I would march through a column in strict order. Other times I would randomly pick out a listing, trusting the universe to choose a winner. Typically, I would have a drink, a pack of cigarettes and an ashtray within reach before making a call.

Sip. Sip. Inhale and exhale smoke. Dial.

"Hello? Is this Mrs. Phipps? My name is Catherine Anderson and I am a paralegal from Simpson and O'Neil. I am in the process of probating a will, and I am trying to locate woman with the maiden name of Phipps born around 1930 in the Midwest. Could that be someone in your family?"

Here is a sample of what I got in response:

"Nobody related to me, sorry." (neutral)

"Wow, how much money?" (greed)

"How did you get my number?" (wary, which got up my hopes, only to be dashed when no other information matched).

After each disappointing call I would draw a heavy black line through the listing, take another sip of my cocktail, and grind out my cigarette. Some days I would stop after only one call. Other times I would force myself through half a dozen or more just to get it over with. Sometimes I had let weeks go by without working on my list. On my twenty-sixth birthday I was so morose I took the day off from work. Surely, Mother Phipps would remember the day I was born, I figured, as I mixed a batch of frothy daiquiris in the blender. It was the perfect day to connect. Mystically, we would be reunited on the day of her labor and my birth. By late afternoon, all I had achieved was slurred speech, a column of names with black lines drawn through them in an increasingly wobbly manner, all the ingredients for a huge hangover, and bout of depression in a darkened room the following day.

My gloom gave way to paranoia by the following month after several other crazed sessions of dialing Phipps. Maybe Miss MacFarland at Catholic Charities had lied. Others in my group discovered that they had been deliberately deceived by adoption agencies to throw them off the track. I needed another source of confirmation for the information I already possessed and new clues to help me advance my search.

Inspiration struck one afternoon in late summer as I sat in my office at work during a lull. What if the law firm that had handled my adoption still had records? My mother had been very certain of the firm's name. I reached for the Chicago yellow pages in the bookcase by the desk and flipped to the attorney listings. There it was. Flynn and O'Reilly, downtown across the street from City Hall. The air directors and announcer were not in the office, so I placed the call immediately before I had a chance to change my mind.

"Mr. Flynn isn't in today. I'll ring Mr. O'Reilly for you," said the secretary. I was stunned. The most I had hoped for was access to records. Who would have thought that one of the original lawyers was still alive and practicing? I quickly composed myself and succinctly explained my situation to the attentive Mr. O'Reilly.

"Now, how long ago was this case, Miss Veto?" he asked when I had finished explaining my curiosity about my origins. His voice rasped and cracked like an old radio.

"I was born in 1949."

"Ah, I see. Well, I don't have those files here. Anything that far back is stored in the basement of my son's real estate office. But I can have my son's secretary send the files over to me. I must warn you, though, that there was a flood a few years back and we lost some of those files. Truthfully, Miss Veto, I don't remember your parents. We used to handle thousands of adoptions a year back in those days. You know, the World War II babies and the boom." I waited out another pause. "What were you looking for?"

I hesitated. I had learned to be wary about answering that question. I also knew not to tell him about my trip to Catholic Charities.

"Oh, well, anything that might be there. I've become interested in my adoption lately and just wondered if there's any of my story around. My folks told me everything they knew, which wasn't much. My mother did give me your name, though, thinking you might have more documentation."

"I see. They know about your . . . curiosity?"

"Oh, yes."

"You must get along well with your parents."

"Yes, indeed. We're very close." The fact that I was telling him the truth; that I loved my parents and had a good relationship with them, did not alleviate my resentment nor staunch the bitter feeling churning in my stomach. I could get information about my own birth and ancestry only if someone in a position of power liked me; deemed me suitable and stable and deserving. As an adoptee, I was in a lifelong audition process to be chosen for the role of my own true self.

"Let me see what we have on file. You can call back Wednesday."

"Thank you, Mr. O'Reilly. I certainly will. By the way, do you think there are any names in there?" I knew it was not cool to appear too anxious, or to tip my hand that I was searching for my birth mother, but I blurted it out anyway.

"Well, your mother had to sign the adoption decree to relinquish her rights to you. Her name should be there. But as they say, a rose by any other name would smell as sweet."

"I beg your pardon?"

"Shakespeare, you know."

"Yes, I know. Well, thanks. I'll call on Wednesday."

Why did a kindly man like O'Reilly, who worked on thousands of adoptions during his career, seem to think that one's name was so unimportant? Maybe Romeo and Juliet did not care in the throes of adolescent passion, but even then, they *knew* their own names, their lifelong identities as Montague and Capulet. And if we are quoting Shakespeare here, how about the anguish of Edmund in *King Lear:* "Why bastard? Wherefore base?" Demonizing "illegitimate" children is an old game. And consider what extreme and bloody behavior Edmund employed to gain the birthright he was denied. Entire cultures revolve around naming ceremonies and the taking and giving of names. Names confer holy and magical powers that define personhood, rights of succession, fates, and nations. Of course, I wanted my own name!

Two days later I called O'Reilly back and was put through to him immediately. He probably was not handling much of a caseload in his semi-retired state.

"Good morning, Miss Veto." His voice was cheery. "I have your file right here on my desk. Let's see. 1945. Robert . . . wait a minute. Do you have a brother?"

"Yes," I replied impatiently, my pen poised over a note pad. "Bob. He's four years older than me."

"Ah, that explains it," muttered O'Reilly. "This must be *his* file. I'm awfully sorry, Miss Veto, but this is the only file we have under that last name. Yours must have been in the group we lost in the flood. We just have your brother's."

I felt sick to my stomach and a chill ran up my spine. Resentment blossomed in my chest. Why was Bob's file so accessible and mine missing? Bob had no curiosity whatsoever about his own birth parents. It just wasn't fair! I took a deep breath to calm myself before replying.

"And there are no other copies of my decree? Anywhere?" I managed to say weakly.

"The court has the only other copy of those records. And they're sealed."

"Yes, I know." I no longer tried to keep the bitterness out of my voice. The stone wall around what I felt to be my right to my own identity was one more manifestation of institutional oppression as far as I was concerned. There was a long pause before O'Reilly spoke again.

"Miss Veto, are you related to Bill Veto?"

"Yes, he was my uncle," I responded, surprised.

"A fine man. I worked with him back when he was a green reporter. He did me favors in his time, many a good turn. The good go young, as they say."

"Yes, it must be seven years now since he died."

There was another pause at the other end of the line.

"Listen, sometimes adoption files are opened if the court is petitioned. Why don't I go across the street and see who's holding the cards these days?"

Once again, the ghost of Uncle Bill hovered over the legal papers of my identity. First it was Sandra Mullen's mining of my name from the microfilm files of *The Daily Law Bulletin* where he had worked, and now an old crony lawyer trying to return a favor.

"That would be terrific. Do you think they'd do it, though? I thought they opened records only in cases of critical medical or psychiatric problems."

There was a chuckle on the other end of the line.

"Officially, yes. But my dear Miss Veto, this *is* Chicago, and more than one old duffer would be happy to do Bill Veto's niece a nice turn, you know?"

"I can't thank you enough for taking the time to help like this."

"Honey, at my age, when you're running out of time in one sense, all you have is time on your hands. I'll get back to you this afternoon." How quickly I spun from despair to celebration, from resentment to gratitude. I was riding a relentless wave that threatened to drown me or offer a safe harbor by turn. I just had to hold on.

He did call back and with the happy news that Judge Amelia Murdock had granted the opening of the file on the following Monday morning. I was transported. The Chicago political buddy machine was churning in my favor. But the euphoria was short lived. Just before I left work on Friday, I had another call from O'Reilly.

"Miss Veto, I'm awfully sorry. I'm afraid your file has been sealed again. Judge Murdock put through the order, but Kelly, the presiding judge, overrode it. He doesn't want *any* records opened since there's such hoopla these days about adoption records. I'm sorry. I truly am sorry."

I felt tears sting my eyes, but my sadness was overshadowed by silent rage. Kelly! I knew about him. He was the one who sealed the records in the county ten years before. I had heard from other adoptees in Yesterday's Children that he was an immovable force and the primary defendant named in the class action suit that had been filed against the state to open the records.

"I see. Well, thanks for taking a crack at it." I was working hard to keep my voice even, to stay polite when inside I was screaming with frustration and an all too familiar disappointment. I came to realize that the sense of entitlement that came so naturally to so many people with fewer gifts and less loving homes than my own was elusive for me. Something about being adopted, for me, meant I had to *earn* everything; nothing was mine by birthright, as I, in truth, had none.

"Wait a minute, Miss Veto. I did talk to the judge, and he'll see you Monday if you'd like. No chance of him changing the order, mind you, but he'll talk to you. Your Uncle Bill did him a few favors in the old days, too."

"Okay. What do I have to lose? I'd like to get a look at him and hear firsthand why I can't have my records." I had already resolved to use up as many sick days at work as I needed to pursue my case.

"Fine. We'll go over together. Meet me at my office Monday at ten."

***

The following Monday morning Pat O'Reilly held my elbow gently as he reached for the handle of the big double doors of smoked glass that opened into the courtroom. He was a big, ruddy-faced Irishman with a thatch of white hair, a sort of Tip O'Neil character with a midwestern twang. Once again, I was dressed in full well-adjusted adoptee drag camel-hair sweater and skirt, a gold crucifix at my throat. Once in the door, O'Reilly nodded to one side, indicating I should take a seat in one of the long pew-like benches.

Court was in session. A well-scrubbed couple in their late thirties stood before the judge. Between them, a young Latino boy about six years old shifted his weight impatiently from side to side. The woman's hand rested lightly on his shoulder in a discrete effort to settle him down. She and her husband had their heads tilted back; eyes raised to the judge on his throne above them. His white hair contrasted handsomely with the black folds of his gown. In the dark hush of the room, the single spotlight on the immaculate, groomed form of Judge Kelly was impressively theatrical. The court shared that dramatic flair with the Catholic Church. I was decades away from appreciating the soothing and necessary side of ritual in faith and law. In my adolescent righteousness I was obsessed with "truth," which I believed should be served naked, with no trimmings, a pure slab of protein to power the system.

O'Reilly conferred with the bailiff at the side table as the judge spoke to the couple. The soon-to-be-parents nodded obediently then cast quick glances at the boy. Obviously, the scene was building to a climax, but I was too far back to hear the words. O'Reilly was making his way back to me from his chat with the bailiff when a sharp crack shot through the room. As Kelly laid down his gavel, the bailiff reached over the rail to hand the boy a sucker. Case settled.

Would this boy come back, fifteen years from today, perhaps to this very courtroom to ask his own probing questions? I must have appeared in such a courtroom. Everyone must have been as nervous and excited and happy with the proceedings as these people were. Bang! Another case concluded, a new name conferred, another family created. Entrance to a bright, happy future through a dark, secret door to be sealed and locked behind the unknowing child.

O'Reilly tapped me on the shoulder. "Time to go. He wants to see you in his chambers." I stumbled out of the pew and fought the old instinct to genuflect. What was the point of making me sit through an adoption case? In my paranoid state I thought there was a conspiracy to chastise me, to try and impress me with the powerful trappings of the law. It did not take much for me to create a story to justify my resentment.

O'Reilly and I took a corridor to the left and followed it to a door at the end with Kelly's name embossed on a brass plate in the center. He gave the wood a sharp tap with his knuckle and opened the door for me into a spacious, sunny room with a large, cluttered desk situated at one end. O'Reilly shook my hand, waved to the judge, and started back down the hall. I had not counted on being left alone and rapidly tried to conceal my confusion. Judge Kelly rose to greet me. He was a short man with chiseled features, lace curtain Irish of the old guard, I figured.

"Now, Miss Veto, what is it that you want to know?"

It was time for another audition. I inhaled slowly and composed my features into what I hoped was an open face graced with a sweet smile.

"Up until a few months ago, Your Honor, I never even thought very much about my adoption. Why should I have?" Imploring, sincere look here. "After all, I have lovely parents and certainly there is no dissatisfaction on my part. Then my boyfriend and I became engaged and, well, we started talking about children." Pause; then shy, downcast eyes. "Suddenly, it became important to know more about my biological past for the sake of our future children."

"I see." A young woman slid a batch of file folders onto the corner of Kelly's desk. "Would you care for some coffee, Miss Veto?"

"Yes, thank you, Your Honor. Black."

"Two, please, Karen." He turned to his secretary then turned his attention back to me. "Please continue."

"Well, I went to my mother, but she had very little information. She told me all she knew years ago. But she did give me the name of Mr. O'Reilly and his partner and suggested I check with them. As you probably know from Mr. O'Reilly, my file was destroyed in the flood in his son's real estate office. So, he approached the court to ask for their copy and here I am." I smiled crookedly.

"I'm sorry to say there usually is little medical information in those files. Most of the babies put up for adoption from your time were healthy and did not carry any serious family disease. But, of course, there could have been exceptions and I must admit, the records could have been better kept. We have altered our procedure, but that's not much help to you, I know."

Kelly was studying me closely but his eyes were kind. Not the authoritarian character I had anticipated. I was in my twenties. I was a product of the sixties and in school when the afterglow of pride left over from World War II turned to bitter rage and shame over Viet Nam. Why had I spent my first twenty years being such a good girl if Americans were not automatically the guys in white hats? I came of age precisely at the time when normal adolescent questioning coincided with a societal upheaval of faith in the "American Way" among the best and the brightest of my generation. All agents of church, state and corporate life were suspect. And yet, within the "system" as we called it with scorn, the secrets of my own identity were buried.

"Also, the court is in a difficult transition now," Kelly continued. "Many adoptees are stridently demanding their files. While many of them are sincere, others are just looking for someone to blame. There is even a group that has started a lawsuit to that end." I concentrated on keeping my face expressionless even though my cheek muscles started to twitch. "You see, the court also has an obligation to the natural mothers who were guaranteed secrecy. Whose rights are foremost? Those of the grown child or of the mother who potentially could suffer from disclosure?"

"Couldn't the court act as a go-between?" This was an idea hotly discussed at Yesterday's Children meetings. Some members wanted this system put into place, while the more radical contingent wanted direct access to their records regardless of the birth mothers' wishes.

"That's an idea we are considering." The judge drew back a few inches. "Of course, it would involve constructing an infrastructure and a good deal of time to work out procedure. But, yes, that is a possibility in the future. In the meantime, we have sealed all the records to protect the greatest number. It is dangerous to start a precedent before all the legalities are decided. I understand your position, though, Miss Veto, and it is legitimate. Let's look in your file and see what we can share."

He reached for a file folder, opened it, and casually scanned down the page. My heart skipped a beat. Once again, I was sitting within a yard of my file, going through all sorts of gyrations to eke out information. Thank God, I did not have a hair-trigger temper.

Kelly's salt and pepper brows furrowed for a moment. He peered at me over the file.

"Hmm. You don't look like a Bruno to me."

"Ah, no. I don't believe so."

"It seems I have the wrong file. One moment, please." He waved to his secretary as she entered the back of the room with the coffee.

"Karen, there's been a mistake with the file. I'll be right back."

He disappeared through the side door as Karen deposited the steaming cup in front of me. I sipped my coffee and fantasized about a Marlboro. Then it hit me. Was this a set up? The judge could not just hand me the file, but did he walk out to leave me alone with it as a sort of favor to the niece of a dear departed colleague?

My eyes raked the desk. Christ, there were so many files lying around. But docket numbers labeled them all and I knew mine by heart. I shot a nervous glance to the side door. Nothing. To the back doorway. Damn. I could see the secretary standing between her desk and a set of file cabinets. She was sure to see me if I stood up and I could not reach any of the files from where I was sitting.

What if this was not a set up? What if I reached for a file that might not be there, got caught, and lost every chance of getting information? Slowly, I rose to my feet and smoothed my skirt as if I just needed to stretch my legs. From my new perspective I could see the files splayed across the desk more clearly. I started to lean toward the desk when I heard footsteps behind me. Frantic, I riveted my eyes to the fish tank along the back wall.

"Would you care for more coffee?"

"Sure, sure. Love some. Ah, great fish there, eh?" I gestured toward the tank. "Tropical?"

"Goldfish," she replied evenly. Was she suspicious? I could not gauge it. I sat down abruptly as my knees gave out. Damn! It took a few minutes to get my breath back to normal after she left the room. I consoled myself with the thought that the file probably was not on the desk anyway. As I was about to try my luck again, Judge Kelly swept back into the room and resumed his seat behind the huge walnut desk.

"Sorry about the delay. The clerks sometimes get confused. But so do I. They swear it's somewhere on my desk." He started to shuffle a pile of folders in front of him. He stopped at the third file. "Ah, here it is. How thoughtless of me."

"It happens to all of us," I responded weakly. It was there all the time.

His eyes took in the first sheet, paused, and continued to the next. After a moment, he looked up at me and adjusted his reading glasses.

"Well, you'll be happy to know that there doesn't seem to be any alarming information here. There is little about your father, other than that he was Italian."

"Yes, I know."

"Your mother is still quite young. That's another reason we can't share too much. She is in the prime of family life now, I imagine. If she were older, maybe we could give more."

"I understand. How old is she?"

"Well, she was nineteen when she had you, so in her midforties. Still a young woman." He smiled warmly. "I could tell you your name, though. It was Alana. Very pretty."

"Yes, my mother told me." I mustered a grateful expression. "I guess the nuns told her my baptized name when they adopted me."

"Oh, I see." He was trying to give me some shred of information without betraying his professional code of ethics. By now he must have figured out that I had not seen the file, if, indeed, he had intended for me to see it at all. At least he had confirmed my mother's age and my name. That made me feel the rest of the information I had gotten from Catholic Charities was true as well. That was something.

"Was she a Chicagoan?" I asked innocently.

"No, from another midwestern city. I can't give you the name. It would be identifying information. Some people go and look, you know. Sorry."

"Oh, well, I wouldn't want you to do anything out of line. I appreciate the position you're in. You can't start a precedent. I understand. I was just curious, as you can imagine."

He was receptive. What the hell. I would go for the big one. I worked myself into a shy, eye-batting pose.

"My fiancé and I were talking about names the other night, and well, I'm rather sentimental. You see, my brother has already named one of his daughters for our mother, so I don't want to repeat that." He nodded along. "So, I was wondering if you could tell me her first name. That wouldn't be identifying now, would it?"

He smiled broadly. Either he believed me or was pleased with the opportunity I gave him to give something without violating the law. In any case, he just nodded.

"Certainly. Her name is Beverly."

The blood rushed to my head. I could not believe it. I had what I needed. Beverly. Somehow I managed a casual thank you. I have no memory of the next five minutes or how I got out of the judge's office. Inside my head a pounding rhythm was building. Beverly. Beverly Phipps. My mother, Beverly. From the Midwest. About forty-five years old. Now she could be found.

***

Three weeks after my meeting with Judge Kelly, I sat behind the locked door of my office at the television station studying a Photostat birth certificate for Beverly Ann Phipps, born September 24, 1930, in Sioux City, Iowa. She was listed as the fifth child of farmer Joshua Phipps and his wife Cecilia Bordeaux Phipps. Everything I had pieced together about my mother over the past two years fit this profile.

One of my Yesterday's Children friends was a social worker. I had rushed to call her when I got home after the session at the court. The very next day she sent out an official request to seven midwestern states for the birth certificate of Beverly Phipps born between 1929–31 for "verification for benefits." As part of the adoptee network, and another gay woman besides, she did not hesitate to risk her professional standards and her job, for that matter, to get the document. Now it was up to me.

I turned down the sound of the television that faced my desk. As Continuity Director, I constantly monitored the breaks between programs to assure that they were executed smoothly. That day's third episode of "Sesame Street" was just starting. I had more than twenty minutes before I had to look up again. I picked up the phone. I had a feeling Beverly Phipps had left Iowa a long time ago, but maybe a brother or cousin had stayed put on the farm.

"Information for Sioux City? Do you have a listing for Joshua Phipps?"

"I have a J. J. Phipps on Bluff Street. Could that be your party?"

"I'll take it." I stared at the number on the pad in front of me. A large flash of yellow crossed the screen. Big Bird. I picked up the phone again and dialed the number.

"Hello?" It was an elderly woman's voice.

"Hello, Mrs. Phipps?"

"Yes?"

"My name is Catherine Anderson and I'm with the law firm of Simpson and O'Neil in Chicago. I am in the process of probating a will and I'm trying to locate a Beverly Phipps born in 1930. Could she possibly be a relative of yours?"

I had made the pitch so many times that I often thought I *was* a paralegal.

"Oh. Let's see. I think Beverly's one of my husband's daughters."

"*Husband's* daughter?"

"Yes. I'm the second Mrs. Phipps. I've never met Beverly myself. She lives in New York, you see."

My heart flipped over in my chest. Was my real grandmother dead? But New York, yes, that made sense, at least in the fantasy I had about my birth mother. She would not hang around an Iowa farm if she were anything like me. I projected restlessness, adventure, and glamour upon her, plus a lot of spunk. The New York residency fit perfectly with any number of the revolving scenarios I had constructed about her over the years.

"Ah, do you happen to have her phone number or address?"

"No, I'm afraid not. Her sister lives near here, though. She might have it."

"Fine. Could I have her name and number, please?"

"I suppose so. It's Mrs. Rebecca Longwood. 756-3738."

"Thank you, Mrs. Phipps. You've been an immense help. I appreciate it."

"You're welcome, dear. Good luck."

Good luck, yes, it was about time for good luck. I was reasonably certain I had the same family listed on the birth certificate in front of me. Now all I needed was confirmation that *that* Beverly Phipps was my mother. The next call could do it; the call to my Aunt Rebecca.

"Hello, is this Mrs. Rebecca Longwood?"

"Yes, who is this?"

My canned speech flowed out on automatic pilot. There was a hesitation at the other end of the line accompanied by crackling static.

"Well, I do have a sister named Beverly who was born in that year," she confirmed finally.

"I see," I urged her on. "Do you happen to know her phone number or address so we could check with her?"

"Who died?"

I caught my breath. "I beg your pardon?"

"I said, who died?"

No one had asked me that before. "I'm sorry, I'm not at liberty to discuss the conditions of the will with anyone but the party named."

"I see. What law firm did you say you are with?"

"Simpson and O'Neil. Randolph Street. Chicago." I gritted my teeth. She was suspicious. Two years later I would stand next to this woman—my aunt—as we leaned on a corral fence in Sioux City, Iowa, watching her daughter Kim saddle up a horse, and learn I was not so clever after all.

"Oh, I guess it couldn't do any harm anymore," Rebecca Longwood sighed. "I haven't seen my sister in many years. We do exchange Christmas cards occasionally. Hold on, I'll have to get my address book."

I tapped a tattoo on my note pad with my pencil.

"Miss Anderson, I'm back. Her address is 123 St. Mark's Place, New York. I don't have the zip."

I froze. I had haunted that seedy neighborhood regularly when I had lived in New York my first year out of college. How many Saturday afternoons had I sat in the St. Mark's Cinema watching vintage films from the thirties and foreign films with illegible subtitles? Had I passed my mother on the grimy streets that always seemed damp in that area; sat next to her at the movies? I knew that neighborhood, all right. I had enough sense to stay out of it at night when drug dealers ruled.

"That's okay, Mrs. Longwood. Do you have her phone number?"

"No, no phone, but her name isn't Phipps anymore. It's Shelton."

"Shelton. Fine. What is her husband's name?"

"Oh, well, she's been divorced for twenty years. I don't even remember anymore."

"Thank you. That shouldn't matter. Oh, and one more thing. Do you happen to know if she lived in Chicago at any time?"

Again, there was a hesitation, followed by a sigh.

"Yes, she was there for a while about twenty-five years ago."

"Thank you, Mrs. Longwood. I appreciate your help."

I sobbed as I replaced the receiver. It had to be her. Everything fit. After two years of musty city offices, institutions, and official red tape that led nowhere. After two years of theatrical performances for bureaucrats and officious defenders of the public good; after two years of the deadly cycle of hope followed by crushing disappointment delivered over the phone by indifferent, anonymous voices.

I could not keep my mind on the job. I scribbled a hasty note to my assistant, fled the cinder block studio, and jumped into my battered blue Volkswagen. I had to get home, pack, and reserve a seat on a flight to New York the next morning. Job, lover, commitments faded from my mind. I had one thought, one obsession: to come face-to-face with Beverly Ann Phipps as quickly as possible.

Yet for all my urgency, I took what was, for me, a strange detour. For some inexplicable reason, the spire of St. Ignatius Church caught my eye. I pulled over to the curb in front of a long flight of stone steps and got out of the car. I barely noticed the frigid wind whipping the dry snow around my ankles. I had not been in a church for years, and yet here I was, being drawn compulsively into the dark recesses of an unfamiliar church.

My footsteps echoed loudly as I walked down the center aisle, past rows of vacant pews. I veered to the left, away from the main altar and the Christ figure hanging from the cross, towards the statue of the Virgin Mary. I dropped to my knees. Tears ran down my cheeks as I looked up at the open-armed figure illuminated by the flickering light given off by red votive candles. She looked down at me with an expression of infinite compassion and tenderness. I knew then that my quest had to do with mothers and a terrible need to be embraced, reunited, and made whole.

Make it be her, I prayed. Make it be her and, please, please let her accept me. She cannot give me away again. If she tries, she will have to gaze into eyes so like her own as she does it. Make her choose me. Set us both free of ghosts and the shadowed past that hides us from each other. Mary, Queen of Heaven, have mercy on us. Mother of All, grant me peace.

Reunions

Six Flights Up

After two years of searching, I was about to meet my birth mother. A slow rain drummed on the roof of the cab as we pulled away from LaGuardia. Smoking was still permitted in cabs back then and I was lighting one after the other as we made our way towards Manhattan via the Triborough Bridge. It was the weekend after New Year's and the city was quiet under the gray drizzle. If luck were with me, within the hour I would look on the woman who had given birth to me.

I was arriving unannounced and, for all I knew, as unwanted now as I had been twenty-five years before. I knew no more about Beverly Ann Phipps Shelton than I had when I hung up the phone after speaking to Rebecca Longwood in Iowa the day before. I had been unable to find a phone listing for Beverly. I debated about writing a letter first to prepare her but decided against it. I did not want to give her a chance to disappear or to build barriers.

I might have decided to cushion the surprise if she had been living in the suburbs or in a small town, but maybe I just tell myself that now as if to suggest I was operating under some sort of logic and concern for my birth mother. Yes, it was a self-centered decision on my part and I doubt anything would have deterred me in my headlong rush to bring the drama of my search to its finale. I wanted to see her pure, unfiltered reaction when recognition crossed her face and she realized she was looking at her own grown, flesh-and-blood daughter.

I did know the Lower East Side, however, and I was not wrong about the non-bourgeois nature of the neighborhood in the pre-gentrified 1970s. Nothing could shock someone living in an area where mutilated corpses of dope dealers hung from swing sets in the park. It was nearly two decades before the area experienced its hip renaissance and performance artists staged smug pieces about the encroachment of Starbucks and Gap.

It took me fifteen minutes to check into a hotel and to jump into another cab. I got out at Cooper Union and headed east. I wanted to walk the last few blocks to calm my nerves and to prepare my approach. I had been so hell-bent on getting to New York, I had not had time to clearly work out my strategy. I was a conspicuous outsider as I walked down St. Mark's Place in my neat gray slacks and sweater and my good suede coat spotted by the fine rain. I suppose I looked like a coed seeking recreational drugs. A few teenagers approached me and mumbled offers, but I shook my head and kept walking.

I came to a full stop in front of number 123, a grime-encrusted, eight-story tenement that differed little from its neighbors. What did I expect? A holy mandorla, a full body halo, glowing around the crumbling brickwork? A fetchingly interesting individual quirk to the entrance to mark its importance?

A group of Black men clustered in front of the liquor store next door started up their "Hey, Baby," chorus. Across the street, a woman huddled in a doorway peering out from under her pile of rags with mad eyes and letting out a piercing wail in counterpoint to the bass throb of the drunken men. She cursed the rain and the rainmaker who called himself a god and the men and me with equal ferocity.

I turned my back to her, lit a cigarette and climbed the worn stone steps to the front door. Only half the rusted mailboxes had names on them, but I was in luck. "B. Shelton" was scrawled on a scrap of dirty paper covered by brittle yellow Scotch tape. I inhaled smoke in short puffs and checked a few other names listed on the boxes. I wanted to leave myself an out if I had the wrong person or I panicked at the last minute. I could always say I was looking for someone else in the building.

It was then that the reality of the situation sunk in. I was visited with doubts and fears that had nothing to do with the very real danger of my physical safety and everything to do with my emotional well-being in encountering my birth mother. At that moment, she was the most powerful person on earth for me and I had yet to lay eyes on her. The anticipation was so great that I knew I would faint if she was not home. I was a projectile in motion towards a target and was powerless to halt my forward thrust to impact.

I flung down the half-smoked cigarette and pushed the Shelton buzzer. Befuddled by the immediate buzzing open of the door, I tripped over the splintered doorjamb into a dark foyer littered with trash. A grimy marble staircase wound up to my left. I took a deep breath of the fetid air and started to climb. By the first landing my breath was coming in gasps. What if it was not her at all? What if it *was* her and she denied me? The odor of urine and rotting garbage filled my nostrils as I trudged on to the second

Beverly Phipps Shelton, birth mother, c. 1960, Tangiers.

landing and then the third when the sound of a door opening above me caused me to pause.

"Who's there?" demanded a man's voice.

I froze. Who, indeed? That is precisely why I was there. "Is Beverly Shelton there?" I called.

"Yeah, who is it?" The voice was guarded.

"Janine Veto," I called back with a nervous laugh. The name would be meaningless to them. I continued to wind my way up the stairs, knowing I was close, within five landings, five spiral turns, to the center of my obsession. I finally rounded the sixth-floor landing and faced a tall, slender teenager with a riotous auburn Afro staring at me from behind a half-opened door. We sized each other up before breaking the silence.

"Is Beverly Shelton in?" I repeated, finally.

Apparently satisfied that I was harmless, the boy nodded.

"Yeah." As he spoke, he swung the door open and stepped back. "Bev?" The apartment opened into the kitchen. Across the room I saw a woman's back. She was putting pins into her heavy, dark auburn hair.

"Are you Beverly *Phipps* Shelton?" I persisted as I stood in the threshold.

The woman turned around to face me. My first reaction was one of crushing disappointment. It was not her. She was shorter than I knew my mother would be. Her hair was darker. Her nose was different.

"Yes . . . and this is my son, Randy." The voice was throaty, verging on the theatrical, and her gesture jerky when she waved towards the boy who had opened the door. I nodded mutely. "What would you like, my dear?"

As she uttered this simple question the room caved in on me, for as she spoke, Beverly Phipps Shelton smiled and put on a pair of glasses. The horn-rimmed frames were identical to my own, and what was more, her smile morphed into an image of my own smile, complete with dimples. Then I took in the suggestion of a widow's peak slightly off center of her forehead and her small hands, so like my own. This was my mother. And if she was my mother, then this tawny teenager was my brother. In my headlong rush to find Beverly, I had never even considered that there might be other children. All this flashed through my mind in the time it took to inhale. I suddenly felt very unsteady on my feet. The blood drained from my face and my heart beat loudly in my ears. Here was the stranger who looked like me. Here stood my mother. I realized she was waiting for me to say something.

"Ah, you really *do* live on the sixth floor," I blurted out.

"Oh, please, come in and sit down." Beverly pointed to one of the rickety metal chairs by a small Formica-topped table against a kitchen wall dappled with rusty stains along spidery cracks. The gooey black adhesive that poked through the worn spots of linoleum stuck to the bottom of my shoes as I crossed the room and slumped into the chair. I lit a defensive cigarette even though I could hardly get enough air to breathe. Beverly shot me a wary look and waited for me to make the first move.

"Ah, this is rather personal." I looked back at Beverly and inclined my head toward the boy. Randy took the hint, shrugged his shoulders, and sauntered down the hall toward the front of the apartment.

"This is, ah, difficult to start." I tried again.

Beverly sat down in the other chrome tube chair and cocked her head. She was dressed in loose black slacks and a black turtleneck sweater that had lost its shape. I stared into her startling blue eyes and tried to find the words to start.

"Does May 14, 1949, in Chicago mean anything to you?" I ventured.

Beverly leaned back, a quizzical look on her face. After a few seconds something clicked behind her eyes and she nodded slowly.

"And, ah, Alana Phipps?" My throat was dry, my voice scratchy. Once again, Beverly nodded in mesmerized slow motion. "Well, when I was born, my . . ."

Beverly's eyes filled with tears. Disbelief. Recognition. I saw each emotion play out across her face. Then her hand shot out, closing over mine resting on the kitchen table.

"Alana!"

I clutched her hand and nodded in mute affirmation. There it was: my mother calling my name. Tears leaked out of the corners of my eyes. Neither of us could speak at first but she recovered more quickly.

"My *dear*, these things aren't supposed to happen. How ever did you find me?"

"Well, it wasn't easy. I couldn't have done it without help from this adoptee's organization, but other people pitched in along the way."

"Wait a minute." She held up a hand to stop me. A faraway look came to her eyes. "I've seen this movie. Ann Blyth. 1950."

"What?" I blinked a few times.

"This movie about an adopted chick from this square family that goes looking for her mother. *Our Very Own* - yeah, that's what it was called."

"I see." I drew a breath.

I have dined out on the story of finding Bev for decades and when I get to this wisecrack almost everyone laughs and says how cool Bev was. Then why does my heart always race at the retelling and disease permeate my system? Only one person ever got it right; a professor of history who, when I delivered my laugh line, softly uttered, "How hurtful and distancing." Exactly.

My appearance seemed to have resurrected her supporting role in a grainy black and white melodrama. It would take many years for me to appreciate that my birth and separation from Bev had inflicted a wound that, along with several other early assaults, had gradually rendered her fit for only bit parts in the scenario of her own life. "Did the movie have a happy ending?" I asked softly.

"I don't remember. I know she ended up back with the squares. I don't know if you'd call that a happy ending. Hold on." She turned and called out in her resounding voice so like Tallulah Bankhead projecting to her fans in the upper balcony. "Randy! Come here and meet your *sister!*"

"You mean he knows?" I was still steeped in middle class midwestern propriety. I was sitting in a tenement kitchen worried that my newly found half-brother needed to be protected from the shame of my birth. Never mind that I was soon to learn that, at fourteen, he had already fathered two children of his own. Despite my having lived through the peace and lovechild era of the sixties, my default reaction was still rooted in my own Villa Park childhood.

"Of course, of course." Beverly waved her hand. "He's always known. We just never figured we'd ever see you."

Randy entered the kitchen with a wide grin on his face and looked me up and down.

"I *thought* you looked familiar."

We all laughed.

"Would you like a drink or something?" asked Beverly.

"I sure would." I had made a promise to myself after my appointment with Judge Kelly a month before not to take a drink until I found my mother. It had been an act of faith and a cautionary move at the same time. I already knew in my early twenties that booze could derail me with false euphoria followed by sickening remorse. To stay focused, I needed to stay sober. The plane trip to New York had been particularly difficult without cocktails. And now I could pull out the stops. I had found my mother.

"Well!" Beverly slapped her knee. "We must send Randy next door for some beer. We have nothing in the place, especially after New Year's. My *dear,* what a night."

Randy thrust the bills Beverly handed him into his jeans and disappeared out the door.

"Come on, let's get comfortable in the other room."

Beverly strode down the hall. I followed her through a bare room that held only an old ironing board. The walls were a streaked, dirty white in need of a paint job, but the floor appeared freshly swept. The ironing board room led into the living room, which was also Beverly's bedroom. The double mattress against the wall under the windows was covered in an Indian print bedspread and sported a few pillows as a backrest for when it was used as a sofa. The Empire State Building was visible through the diamond-shaped grid of the rusty security gate covering the windows. I jumped back a step when I saw a man lying on his side on the floor across the room.

"Wake up, Choco, and meet my *daughter*." Beverly nudged him with her foot as she passed him on her way to the floor sofa.

Choco blinked a few times to get his bearings, then broke into a full smile. Although his eyes were bloodshot and had an unhealthy yellow cast, he was a handsome Black man of around forty. He, too, was dressed all in black.

"Ah, don't you kid me before lunch now, Beverly. Who she?" he asked amiably.

"No, really, Choco. It's true."

Once our story sunk in, he insisted on hearing every detail of the search. I followed Bev's lead and sat down on the mattress across from Choco and leaned gingerly back against the wall. I had a tough time making out Choco's thick Cuban accent, but gradually got into the cadence of his speech. Randy returned as I was winding up the shortened version of my search story, and he set two six packs of beer on the floor in the center of the room.

"Hey, so how's the family, eh? The guys at the liquor store are having a great time with this one, you know?" Randy turned to me as he settled onto the floor in the corner opposite Choco. "They sure noticed you when you came in, but they wouldn't believe that you were my sister. They said, 'Why boy, that's a *white* girl.' And I just said that you were from the days before Bev got educated."

"Pretty good, Randy." Choco slapped his knee and reached for a beer. "I like that one fine. Maybe you not so dumb, eh?"

Randy glared at Choco and strode over to the phone that sat on the floor in the ironing board room to call his girlfriend and tell her about his new sister. Beverly tapped me on the shoulder.

"Alana, dear, would you please reach under that pillow and hand me my pouch?"

I leaned forward, reached behind my back, and felt something soft. I pulled out a floral-patterned jewelry pouch with frayed pink silk piping and handed it to Beverly. She deftly untied the string and drew out two ready-made joints and a bag of grass. I was feeling more and more like one of the squares as time went on. Although I smoked weed a few times during college, it had never been a habit. I found out very quickly that smoking grass while I was drinking led to instant blackouts that cut an evening way too short. But this was my mother, and to refuse would be impolite, I reasoned, so I took a healthy toke and washed it down with my beer. This was one day I knew I would never forget, even with the grass.

"Beverly, I wanted to ask you something," I said as I settled into the cushion, feigning an ease I had yet to achieve. "Why the name Alana?"

"Well," Beverly nodded slowly as she took a toke, "in the middle of Iowa there was this cool chick named Alana. It was the most un-Iowa name I had ever heard of. So, you got it," she hissed, holding her breath.

"I know what you mean. The damned Midwest. "

Beverly waved her arm. "I mean, my *dear*, even after years in New York, I was afraid people would guess I wasn't from the East. Want to hear my nightmare?"

Choco chuckled, drained his beer and reached for another. Randy had rejoined us and was sipping on his in the opposite corner.

"Well, I always thought one day I'd land at Orly in Paris, just so cool and international, and chic. Then, as I'm walking off the plane and down that flight of stairs, someone points at me from the crowd and exclaims in the world's loudest stage whisper, 'Look! Sioux City, Iowa!' I mean, I would absolutely die."

As Beverly collapsed on the mattress next to me in mock devastation, Choco got up and headed for the phone.

"Hallo, Chris. Where Little Chris? Wake him up and tell him his sister want to talk to him." Choco flashed me a big grin from the other room. Beverly pulled out of her mock swoon to explain.

"Oh, Chris is your other brother. He's twenty-one. Lives with his father on 45th Street in the studio. In fact, he just moved out a few days ago."

Choco waved me over and handed me the phone.

"Hello? Who is this?" The voice on the other end was slow and sleepy.

"Chris—My name is Janine. I'm your sister, I guess. I just found Beverly today. Ah, sorry for waking you up."

"Oh, no, it's okay. Unbelievable. Thought we'd never see *you*. I'll be over in an hour. Unbelievable."

I handed the phone back to Choco and accepted another beer. The next hour produced a hodgepodge of stories that I tried to fit into some sort of chronology. Bev had worked as an editor for two literary presses, wrote volumes of prose she then destroyed, spent two years in Tangiers (something to do with having to get out of New York fast because of a bad drug deal), covered the '60s music scene for *Down Beat* and *Billboard*, and was one of the two hundred reporters at JFK airport 1964 when the Beatles arrived for their first US tour. There was also a stint as manager of a porno bookstore. There were stories of the Beat years and cross-country trips on motorcycles with a dizzy array of different men. I figured out that Big Chris had fathered my brother Chris, but not Randy, and that Choco was not Randy's father, either. The beer, the dope, the shock all conspired to make the stories even more confusing. At some point I dove in with my own tales and thrust my file at Bev for her inspection.

"Here. Here's all the paraphernalia, all the detective clues for 'The Search.'"

Beverly turned the pages with a jerky motion. She examined the scraps of paper, the ripped-out phone book pages, the receipts for birth, marriage, and death certificates.

"What's this?" Beverly held up five neatly typed pages. I blushed.

"Oh, a poem I wrote five years ago when I first realized I needed to find you."

I turned away as Beverly read "Mama One, Mama, Too" and nervously opened another beer. Randy had obligingly gone on another beer run when we were running short.

"Alana." Beverly's voice was hushed. "May I keep this? You *are* a poet." Beverly looked proud and pained all at once.

"Sure. Keep it. And borrow the file if you'd like. Guess I don't need it anymore. And a copy of your birth certificate is in there, too, in case you need a spare." I was both pleased and embarrassed at her vetting of my literary aspirations. Beverly gave Randy a kick.

"Get me those old photographs, would you, my dear? I've lost most of the photos from all the moves," she explained, "but I should have some left. Maybe you'd like to see them?"

"Very much."

Randy spilled the contents of a wrinkled brown envelope across the Indian print bedspread. We pawed through them, sorting out the pictures of Beverly. Amazed, I stared long and hard at one black-and-white snapshot. She looked so much like me—the way she held her cigarette, the angle of her body. I still had not recovered from the shock of seeing a blood relative who looked like me. Yes, and not only looked like me, but had similar talents and interests and fantasies.

"Yes." Beverly bent over another photo, tapping it with the pinky finger of the hand that held her cigarette. "This one was taken in the Village shortly before my dragon lady period."

"What?" I blinked several times. The gush of information, the morphing form of this woman from one form into another was making my head spin.

Beverly made a sweeping gesture with her smoldering Gauloise. "Oh, for a while I dyed my hair jet black and wore that white rice paper makeup and very red lipstick and those mandarin collars."

"Oh, I see." I felt like the square "nephew" (who turns out to be the son) of the eccentric relative in Graham Greene's *Travels with My Aunt*. Yes, I wanted this, this heritage of bohemia and chaos to put beside the ordered Veto existence. Somewhere, between these two poles of being, my own true center would find its fulcrum, the still point in my turning world, as T. S. Eliot would have it.

"I suppose you'd like to know about your father?" Beverly blurted.

I gasped. Everyone in the adoption group said the natural mothers were reluctant to talk about the men who had fathered the children they gave away. The memory was usually too painful or bitter.

"Sure, Beverly, if you're comfortable talking about him."

"What's to be uncomfortable about? Not that the whole thing matters, my dear. *I* have the strong genes. Just look at the pictures of the boys when they were small on our way to Tangiers." She pushed a snapshot towards me that showed the two solemn-faced boys on a dock. They looked to be about four and ten years old. "I mean, I passed them for white when I had to for safety's sake with no problem at all." She was right. Randy even had blond hair.

"Well, where should I start?" Beverly inhaled a toke and leaned back against the wall under the barred windows. "You'd think that living on the farm I would know how things worked. But I was *so* naive. Right after high school I figured I had to get out of Sioux City. No more explanation needed on that one, right? My sister, Marie the Good, and her husband Rocky lived in Wilmette near big bad Chicago, so I caught the train the day after graduation. I was going to stay with them for the summer and earn a little extra bread before going to the University of Iowa in the fall."

I took another toke on the joint Beverly handed me. I was thrilled. The greatest writing school in the country was in Iowa and my mother had been there with the legends! Okay, so my bent for literature came from her for sure. I was dazed. Choco was starting to doze off in his corner; Randy bent over a sketchpad, drawing diligently with colored pencils. Bev and I lapsed into our own private world, which was fine with me

"I met this incredibly good-looking young Italian in a bar who played pro baseball or something like that. I should have known to watch out. He carried a picture of himself in his Air Force uniform all spattered with medals."

"Too much," I nodded, assuming her hipster view of military men.

"Yeah, Iowa stupid. Anyway, it was warm, so he asked if I'd like to take a walk. I said 'sure.' A little way from the bar he pointed to a big white house and said how he grew up there and his parents still lived there. It was late and he didn't think we should drop in. So, we sat under the apple tree, for chrissakes, and one thing led to another, as they say in polite movies. Of course, I didn't have a clue. A few months later I turned up pregnant."

"You're kidding!" It seemed so incongruous to me, so Garden of Eden somehow.

"No, my dear, I'm not kidding. Isn't that a Midwestern expression?"

"My god, what are the odds on that? Jesus, I was practically a virgin birth."

"My dear," Beverly pressed one hand to her bosom. "The closest thing to it on this earth, if you don't count pre-puberty."

"Well, then he didn't know about you being pregnant or anything?"

"No, never. Never saw him again. His name is Evo Mini, if you can believe that. If you track him down, he probably won't even remember me. And like I said, I had the strong genes, anyway."

"Didn't you try to get in touch with him, to tell him?"

"My dear, I didn't know the man well enough to talk about such intimate things. He probably wouldn't have believed me anyhow. Men never do. They love to have virgins but never want to take responsibility. I learned that early."

"Was he fair?"

"Fair enough, I guess, considering, I . . . oh, you mean *light*. No, he was more darkish. You probably got your fairness from my mother. She was French and had this ever so white skin. Thank god you didn't get my nose. That's the Indian."

"The what?"

"The Indian. I think my grandmother on my father's side was Sioux, though old Esther never came right out and said much about it. See the nose?" Beverly offered her profile. "Which makes you one-eighth Indian."

"They never mentioned that to me at Catholic Charities."

Beverly snorted. "I wasn't *that* stupid. If I told those tight asses that you had Indian blood, you never would have been adopted. Not in 1949, my dear. They're still racist, I'm sure, but they can't be as choosy anymore."

Not to have been adopted! Would the Indian blood have made a difference to the Vetos? Suddenly, I remembered all the comments about "drunken, lazy Indians" that lived on the reservation near their Wisconsin home. No, they probably wouldn't have wanted me if they had known. They made such a point of asking for a "light" baby girl. Visions of myself as an orphan in a Dickensian hell rose before me.

"If you hate them so much, Beverly, why did you go to Catholic Charities?"

"Youth, my dear. And naiveté. You can imagine my surprise when I learned I was pregnant. My family completely freaked out except for Marie and Rocky. I mean, my mother. Whew! By that time, she was a fanatic Catholic. You know the type. I mean, she had me pegged for the unredeemed whore from the start. Trouble is, I never ran into Jesus Christ to inspire me to change my ways." Beverly let out a whoop, in appreciation of her own joke.

"Yes, she was one for religion, she was. She'd line us up each night before bed when we were kids. Got us right down on our knees to pray. And dragged us to church every Sunday. I mean, she'd even *try* to drive to get us there. We almost made it to heaven early the crazy way she drove that old Ford. Anyway, she didn't want anything to do with me, her tainted daughter, once the evidence started to show." A pained look passed across Beverly's face. "You don't do that. Family isn't supposed to do that." She took a drag on her joint.

"But Marie and Rocky, they were just great. They even offered to raise the kid with me. They had two of their own at the time, but we figured that wouldn't be the best for either me or the—I mean, *you.* So they talked to their priest and he made the arrangements for me to go to Catholic Charities. Ever see *Bells of St. Mary's*? Filthy propaganda. Wasn't like that at all. Only good thing was that I had plenty of time to read. Started *Magic Mountain* but that dreary sanatorium reminded me too much of the home. Got through *Raintree County*, though. Ever see the movie with Elizabeth Taylor?"

I shook my head. All this was too much and yet not nearly enough. All my life I had hungered for the story of this other family. My vague fantasies were being recast and projected onto a huge Technicolor screen of images pouring from this woman, this stranger, my mother.

"Anyway, you'd think I'd learn, but a year later I did it again."

"Did what again?"

"I had another daughter—in Miami. This time it was handled privately. I even made a little extra bread on that one. Bought a great red suit with a purse and shoes to match. It was fabulous."

"Another daughter. Where is she?" I was reaching my limit of comprehension. My delight with Bev's unconventionality was clouding over. I was horrified at how casually she could toss off the story of my lost sister because it just as easily could have been me. Me, exchanged for a new outfit rather than being put into the care of nuns. I was unprepared for the backlash, the havoc this flood of information would unleash on me. There were no studies then about the impact of reunions. I could not know that upon my return to Chicago I would descend into a mental state which would render me incapable of concentrating on any topic for more than two minutes. I pulled up my socks enough to find a therapist to help me integrate the fragments of my newly claimed birthright over the following two years. The full portrait of family was a two-thousand-piece jigsaw puzzle I was trying to assemble and I had not even found all the border pieces yet. I had new pieces to play with but did not know yet where they fit into the overall picture. As an adoptee, you do not get the cover of the box to use as a guide.

"Oh, she was adopted, too. All I know is that she was raised in a Jewish dentist's family in New Jersey. Her father was Jewish."

I was almost afraid to ask the next question of the fertile Beverly.

"Ah, is that all the children then?"

"Yes. I did get pregnant in North Africa by my Arab lover who pulled out my loop, the bastard. He was convinced that all Americans were rich and if he made me pregnant and I married him he would never have to work again. I had an abortion from this French butcher, but that's another story. By then I couldn't handle more than the boys. Boys are so much easier to raise than girls."

"Oh, yeah?" I slowly lowered the can of beer from my lips. Another clue on why I was given away. Had I been a boy, would she have kept me? Were boys to be kept and girls given away, like in old China? A man's woman. Yes, that is what she was. I was about to protest when I felt other eyes on me. A young man stood across the room staring at me.

"Chris, this is your sister Alana-Janine," sang out Beverly, waving her hand.

He inclined his head toward me, blinking behind the thick lenses of his black horn-rimmed glasses. He was about my height but built thicker. His black hair was wavy and his smoky skin was dotted with freckles across the bridge of his broad nose. A quick scan and I decided that we did not look like brother and sister.

"Hello, Janine." His tone was even and strangely formal in the bare, Beat pad.

"Chris. Hello." At a loss for words, I held up a can of beer. "Would you like one?"

"No, thank you. I just got up. I'm going to fix myself some breakfast. Excuse me." He held my gaze for a moment, and then turned back towards the kitchen. His studied movements were a direct contrast to the frenetic gesturing of both Beverly and Randy.

"Oh, that Chris. He's *so* serious. Lives in his head. Fucks twice a year. Writes all the time. He must have trunkloads of the stuff, but he never lets me see any of it. And reads Balzac. *Adores* Balzac. Randy, dear, here. Take Alana's poem to him, see what he thinks."

"He's a writer, then?" My hopes were reignited. Maybe my new brother was a soul mate.

"Well, of sorts. But he works at the *Daily News* as head of the copy boys. No ambition for journalism. Refuses every promotion. Just saves his money and takes off for Africa on jaunts. Well, at least he did when I had good jobs in publishing and could give him some extra bread. It doesn't matter. He does just fine living with his father in that big loft. He's a sculptor, Big Chris. Little Chris plays the sax. Good at that, too, but no ambition." She laughed. "I should talk. I once stayed cooped up here for two years watching old movies, my dear, and staying stoned. It's so good *you've* done something."

I drained the last of my beer. I supposed Beverly meant completing college and holding jobs, most of which I viewed with complete indifference. Maybe she had just as much fantasy going about me as I had about her. Besides publishing a few poems, I had yet to do anything I considered worthwhile. Except this. Except this long fight against polite society that told me I had no right to find Beverly, no right to hear the story that was unfolding before me.

"Want another beer, Beverly?" I stood up and stretched.

"Love one."

I made my way to the kitchen, a little shaky on my legs, and found Chris studiously frying bacon and eggs.

"Your poem is good. I like it very much. Powerful."

"Thank you, Chris." I could feel myself blush again. It was one thing to show Bev the poem and another for this unknown brother to deliver a critique. And yet, I wanted his approval and acceptance, too. As a writer more than a sister at that point. "I wrote it five years ago when I was twenty-one. Your age now, right? Objectively, I know it needs a lot of tightening up. But I haven't done it. It's like a blueprint of my state of mind at the time."

Chris nodded as if it made perfect sense to him. He opened his mouth to speak, caught himself, and frowned slightly as he poked the bacon.

"What is it?"

"You know, when I walked into that room and saw you, well, I became a child again." He laid down the fork and looked me straight in the face. "I saw you and I saw Beverly in a thousand ways. Even your gestures. My God. The way Beverly used to be."

I looked at Chris with a sense of foreboding. He had the solemn demeanor of an aged sage that sat oddly on a boy just out of his teens.

"How she *used* to be? Was that before she stayed cooped up here for two years?"

"Yes, that and before she had all her teeth pulled and the false ones put in. That changed her physically." In my euphoria of finding similar features in Bev's face I had not considered how worn that face was for a woman in her forties until Chris mentioned it. My mother, Marie Veto, was twenty-five years older than Bev and looked a hell of a lot better.

"But you're talking about more than teeth, aren't you?" I prompted Chris to go on. He picked up the fork and lifted the bacon on to a folded paper towel to blot the grease.

"Can't you see? Bev's an alcoholic, a speed freak. She's been doing booze and pills since before I was born. By rights, she should have been dead years ago. Most of her friends are."

"My God." I must have turned white on the spot. Chris slipped the eggs onto a plate and set it carefully on the table.

"I couldn't watch it anymore. My father's no prize, either, but for right now, he's easier to deal with."

"And Choco?"

"And Choco," Chris sneered. "Oh, he's been around quite a while. Broken-down boxer, full-time alkie, and part-time con man. He's taught Randy how to pick a lock in under twenty seconds. Valuable man, that Choco."

Chris speared his eggs into his mouth and chewed purposefully. I stood as still as a sentry, the cold beers numbing my hands.

"Can I talk to you later?" I wanted to talk to him in private, to round out the story.

"Certainly. Get the number from Beverly or Randy. Look, I really am glad to meet you. It's important that someone was saved." He turned back to his breakfast, methodically eating his way neatly across the plate. I rushed out of the kitchen and back to the front room. Beverly hooted at my return.

"I gave you up for dead, my dear. What's the matter? Young Dostoevsky talk you into suicide yet?"

I laughed nervously as I handed Beverly a beer. Ironically, it would be Randy, and not Chris, who would become the suicide in the family, although Chris did give it a half-hearted attempt in a halfway house in Florida that couldn't match the sad and flamboyant final exit staged by his brother.

"Hardly. But I am getting tired."

"Well, I hope you're going to stay here."

"I've got a hotel room. All paid." I tried to toss it off lightly. "Didn't know what kind of reception I was going to get."

Beverly lit another joint.

"You're family, my dear. The place is yours. Do what you want."

I looked around. The late afternoon sun shone through the bars highlighting a grease stain on the wall the shape of Viet Nam. I needed to be by myself to get my protoplasm back into the shape of my skin. My edges had been blurred the past several hours, the vital juices oozing away from me into this new primal pool.

"How about tomorrow morning?" I offered to Bev. "Brunch. Meet you at Sheridan Square, eleven o'clock, okay?"

Beverly grinned. "Gawd, haven't been over to the West Village in ages. Used to live there, too. Sure. Let's be chic, my dear."

I placed my untouched beer on the floor and reached for my coat. I knew better than to be out on those streets alone past dark. In the 1970s, cabs didn't cruise the neighborhood looking for fares. I said my good-byes and spiraled down the dark staircase into the street.

***

The wind gusted in near Chicago-like force through Sheridan Square the next morning. I searched the intersection for signs of Beverly. A figure caught my attention. Was it Beverly? I shook my hangover-afflicted head and tried to focus my eyes. It was Beverly, all right, in slacks, a turtleneck, coat and boots with her long henna hair loose down her back. I looked down at my own attire—turtleneck, coat, boots, my long hair whipping around my face in the wind. Who was intruding in whose fantasy?

Beverly caught sight of me and waved stiffly, flicking her cigarette at the same time. I stepped off the curb to meet her halfway across the intersection. Bev's face broke into a wide grin.

"Well, dear, did you sleep well?"

"The minute I hit the bed. I must have been exhausted."

"Good, good." Beverly spun around, jerking her head. "Haven't been here in ages. Things have changed. I don't go out much anymore. Just to the corner to catch the First Avenue bus to work. Whee!" Then again, the nervous laugh.

Damn, I thought. Must be the speed. Beverly was wound tight, her gestures like sparks from an ever-burning body. What grace allowed me to flourish and her to disintegrate? Was it the nurturing love of my parents, the cruel era before feminist consciousness that gave women ground to stand upon, the irreparable wounding of a woman who gives away her babies, or a brew of all the above?

"Ah, work? Where do you work?" We walked down the street in matched stride. Beverly looked embarrassed.

"My dear, I ran out of money and clever schemes for the welfare people about two years ago, so I was forced into honest labor." She crossed herself as if in a confessional. "I edit journals for a think tank of international electronic engineers, across the street from the UN. Unbelievably dreary. Only about five people in the world can read the damn things."

I smiled. Well, she must have enough brains left to hold that together. Maybe

Chris was embellishing a bit.

"I can just imagine."

"Oh, I make it through, all right." Beverly laughed. "I just pretend I'm in a Forties movie. All those uptight and buttoned-down types almost look in character then. I go to work in my hip Joan Crawford fake fur and wave my cigarettes like Bette Davis. They give me space, I'll tell you. Only I couldn't stand to wear those high-heeled fuck-me-pumps. I lose a lot of effectiveness when I burst from the elevator in my Hush Puppies."

I laughed again and felt the tension gradually ease away. Beverly gestured to a place two doors up the street.

"Let's go in there. I'm freezing my ass off."

The restaurant walls were paneled with a warm wood punctuated with large panes of glass to let in the light. We wove our way between large potted plants to a table at the back overlooking a narrow street. Sunday in the Village, casual style, with people in sweaters, smoking pipes and reading papers. It was an image that appealed to both our fantasy lives.

"Bloody Mary?" I asked.

"Oh, yes. That's so *brunch*."

We sipped our drinks and lit cigarettes. I tried one of Bev's Gauloise. My dream and reality intertwined in the rising smoke. Childhood fantasies of the Village and the literary life merged with this woman sitting across from me wearing my own older, more abused face and body. The blood knows, I whispered to myself. She gave me her hair, her cheekbones, her hands, her brains and her yearnings. Then she gave me away.

Beverly seemed to catch my mood as she stopped in mid-sentence to gaze at me head on.

"My dear. I never doubted I did the right thing giving you up. It was better for everyone. But one thing. I mean, I *know* I have these incredibly strong genes, and well, I know any child of mine wouldn't be content leading a straight, square life. I can see you've got a mind and loads of social outrage against the fucking system. I just always wondered; were you allowed to be yourself? Were you put down for being different?"

I reached my hand across the table and patted Beverly's wrist.

"Beverly, my parents were—are—very loving people. They were always so proud of me and really didn't try to tell me what to do. I'm not saying that they really *understood* me, but they sure did love me. I've got no complaints. They were, or *are*, wonderful."

"Good, good. That's all I wanted to know. Because you seem okay now. Probably smart for steering clear of men and sticking to women."

"How, when . . . I didn't say anything about that."

"You didn't have to," hooted Beverly. "Listen, I've been around. You had plenty of chance yesterday to jump in with stories about your man. You never did. And you don't come across as the virginal type, either. Simple deduction, my dear."

"I'm that transparent?"

"Now, now," cooed Beverly. "I've tried women, too. Lived with a wonderful dyke for a year when the boys were babies. But you need to make decisions—and get your protection. So, I made my choice. I'm not so sure if that was smart now or not." Beverly laughed abruptly and lit another Gauloise.

Once again, I was stunned to silence. I realized that Beverly was trying to make me comfortable, but at the same time, she revealed a severe lack of certainty about herself. Beverly wanted me to approve of her, to condone all her decisions and rebellions through the years. When a woman gives away a child, she does not foresee the day she will gaze into a grown woman's eyes and feel a panic, a primal need to build a bridge across the dark chasm of years yawning between them. The shock of meeting was a two-way street, maybe more like a head-on collision on the separate one-way streets of our lives.

We were not mother and daughter; not yet, and maybe never. Beverly had relinquished that privilege as far as I was concerned. I had a mother in Chicago. But there was blood in common, there were echoes, there were broken bits, fragments in each other that we picked up and compared to what was shattered inside of each us.

In many ways, my search had just begun. I did not know that for an adoptee, the forging of a coherent self would be the journey of a lifetime.

Naturally, Mother

1.

I looked for you

spinning the wheel of my horoscope
I lied for you in court chambers
I performed for your benefit in Catholic charities

But you were always with me
every time I loved and left
each time I put my life in suitcases

as I watch the coupling of friends
and know I cannot follow

envying the simple faith of the world's majority

with the clairvoyance of daughters
I wrote you five years ago

knowing even then
I was writing myself

2.

No wonder you now wear watches
synchronize every clock
panic when someone seems unconcerned

We are all fleshed out pivots of your time

I am here
but only because discreet phone numbers
were not yet published in underground papers

My sister you sold to Miami Jews
for red shoes and a purse to match
The boys you kept
hoping it would be easier
not to raise your own reincarnation
and the nameless one
decomposing somewhere in North Africa

the final ticking under your heart

Freud aside, all our fathers
do not matter
A woman bleeds through her mother

3.

So tempting to stop sailing

retire to a Zen simple room
washed ashore on contemplative rocks
safe from the questions of waves

It is not us

We get sweaty grappling with this life
there is no hope of approval
no safe dry dock
I forced your gaze back, mine inward

But we will not drown

We are buoyed by our own messy faith;
we love

Beverly with her son Chris Shelton and unidentified man, c.1958, New York.

Father's Day

"Hey, babe, this is Evo! Unbelievable. Tell me everything," exclaimed the husky voice on the phone.

"I'll try," I sputtered. He must have called immediately after reading the letter I had sent him two days earlier announcing my existence couched with assurances that I did not want anything from him other than a conversation. He called every night for a week. Then a package arrived with photos of him as a dashing young man, copies of his military awards, articles about his sports promotion, and a round-trip ticket to Denver. Wow. This guy was a man of action.

Compared with the agonies I endured on my journey towards Bev, finding Evo was ridiculously easy. I had him located the very day I started to look for him. But that was months after meeting Bev. It had taken me a long time to process the flood of emotions and for a long time I could not entertain the thought of looking for my other missing parent. Initial euphoria at finding Bev gave way to depression and what I can only characterize as a nervous breakdown. I lost fifteen pounds in three weeks as well as the ability to perform even the most routine daily tasks. Sentence completion had become a challenge. I could not concentrate for more than a few minutes at a time and asked for a leave of absence from work. When it was denied, I quit.

With no job and only my unemployment checks for income, I gave up my apartment on Chicago's far north side and moved to a somewhat seedy studio apartment building in a former hotel in a good neighborhood on the near north across the street from Lincoln Park. I needed time and therapy to get back on track.

By the fall, which always seems like a time of new beginnings to me, I was ready to contact the dashing war hero that blew through Bev's life in the summer of 1948. The urge was not as urgent or fraught as when I was hunting down Bev, especially since he had no idea that I even existed and therefore did not have a part in giving me away. I wanted to find him to round out the picture of myself, to understand what his DNA might have contributed to my attributes and failings. I knew his name and that his parents had lived in Highwood, an Italian enclave north of Chicago. With my well-honed skills at tracking missing persons I was confident I could locate him. Once again, I used the ruse of posing as a paralegal gathering information for a will in probate. I opened a north shore suburban phone book on the hollow core door resting on two file cabinets that I used as a desk and found several Minis.

Evo Mini, birth father, with son Danny, who he thinks is the eldest child, c. 1954.

On my first call the woman who answered was quick to say that while no Evo lived there, she cheerfully volunteered, "Oh, that Evo is Julia Nardini's boy. She's in Highwood. Her husband is Angelo." It was that easy. Fortified by a cup of coffee and cigarette, I placed the call to the Nardini's. A sweet-voiced woman, who happened to be my grandmother, was more than happy to give me her son's address and phone number in Denver. I longed to speak more openly with her but I wasn't sure how she would take to acquiring a new granddaughter, and I also believed that it was Evo's decision about how and when he would tell her. That is, if he accepted what I had to say at all.

The immediate phone call and plane ticket hurled me towards my next reunion. Two weeks later I found myself chain smoking in the passenger seat of a green Chevy sedan next to Carol, Evo's wife, driving through the sprawl of the Denver suburbs. I had expected to see Evo himself at the gate, but instead

I was greeted by a slender, blond woman dressed in a blue parka and stretch pants. Beside her a girl in brilliant red and green was bouncing and waving at me madly.

I deeply inhaled the crystalline air as we walked to the parking lot and turned to take in the beauty of the jagged mountains that ringed the city before I settled in for the drive. During our trip Carol and I made awkward small talk and smoked one cigarette after another as Kelly, my newly acquired eleven-year-old sister, bounced in the back seat wearing my tan fedora down around the bridge of her nose. She was thrilled that at last she had a big sister after coping with five older brothers and had already extracted a promise from me to drive her to a slumber party the next night to show me off to her friends.

"Look," I finally said to Carol. "I know this has got to be a little strange for you and your family. I really don't want to disrupt anything or cause trouble."

"That's real nice of you to say that, honey," she said, issuing an audible sigh. "It's been a little hectic, what with Evo away so much the past few months getting the club ready and all."

"And then coming home each night to call me the past few weeks, I'm sure didn't help."

"Right," she laughed, and then under her breath, almost as if to herself rather than to me. "Sometimes there just doesn't seem to be enough of him to go around."

We pulled into a small shopping area and parked the car in the middle of a swarm of trucks and vans loaded with lumber and electrical equipment. Three men were hoisting a pink neon sign with the name "The Speakeasy" into place with a crane. We followed two men rolling a spool of electrical cable into a tan brick building with a black shingle overhang.

It took a moment for my eyes to adjust to the dark when we entered. Harsh illumination from bare bulbs and work lights dotted the space. A few chandeliers at the side gave off a glittery glow. The smell of freshly cut wood filled the air.

I spotted him leaning over a table set in the middle of the room, jabbing a blueprint with his forefinger as he gave instructions to a young man next to him. His dark wavy hair was peppered with grey, but he was undoubtedly the same man who posed so seductively in the World War II era snapshot dressed in his Air Force uniform. Clad in khaki work pants and a light blue shirt open at the throat, he moved with the easy grace of an athlete. Ah, I thought. That is where I get the knack for sports.

"Daddy, she's here!" shouted Kelly above the sharp zing of a power saw.

Evo looked up and placed a hand on the young man's shoulder to stop the conversation. His dark, slightly slanted eyes found me. Breaking into a wide smile he stepped forward with open arms.

"Hey, Babe. Come here."

I tiptoed through the piles of sawdust and discarded nails and into his arms. He drew me close against his muscular chest and squeezed until I was short of breath.

"You're kind of tall, aren't you?" he said, releasing his grip and holding me out at arm's length.

"Bev's side of the family, I guess. She has a few very tall brothers."

"Could be. But you're good-looking like me," he teased. He jerked his head to indicate the hubbub that surrounded them. "Well, what do you think of your old man, huh? You said you wanted to get to know me. Here it is."

"Very impressive. You seem to like to run your own show."

"Is there another way?" Evo took me by the arm for a tour. "This is a real first-class operation here. A white piano goes over here with a classy singer. Lots of plants. Crystal. Blow ups here in the lounge from old Chicago newspapers. You know, Capone, the St. Valentine's Day Massacre. Everything just like in the Roaring Twenties. Even a big glass ball over here to catch the light."

"Sort of Chicago West with mountains, eh?"

"Why not? The old hometown isn't so bad. My Mama—your Nonna—is still there, right? Wait 'til you meet her, she's a real doll. She'll make you some ravioli and zampone that's out of this world. Wish I could get her out here to cook for me. Hey, it's lunch time. You hungry? We'll go over to the 'Time Out' and we can get acquainted. Carol and Kelly can pick you up there later. What do you say?"

Caught up in the whirlwind that was Evo, I was swept towards the door. He exuded good will, acceptance, and enthusiasm. What more could I ask? He even implied I would be embraced by the only grandmother I was to ever know. Lucky. I was lucky. And breathless.

Evo poured out his abbreviated biography during our short drive as I struggled to keep up with the stories. His tales were as colorful as Bev's but without the scary parts. After the war he had become a minor league baseball player in the Midwest and had a twenty-five-year career in the Air Force with several years as athletic director in Hawaii. When he told me the dates he lived there, I was struck by the fact that I had lived on the other side of the Koolau Mountains in Oahu at the very same time. It was uncanny how the two places I had lived outside the Midwest were where my unknown birth parents were living. My excitement at the coincidence coincided with a growing dread about the tyranny of genes. Looking back on choices that I had believed were mine alone, I was now prompted to consider there was a force of magnetism at work that drew me to both Bev and Evo. Did I really want to belong to them this much? Did I have a choice?

"And here's where my new life started after the Air Force," he announced as he pulled into the large parking lot that surrounded "Evo's Time Out." Goal posts were positioned on either end of the parking lot, which was marked off with wide white stripes across the black top every five yards in imitation of a football field. "You like it? The other places I fix up to sell. The Time Out is home. It's for guys like me who are crazy about sports. Come on, I'll show you."

The restaurant was Valhalla for jocks. Baseball pennants from the Chicago Cubs, New York Yankees, St. Louis Cardinals, and other major league baseball teams studded the woodpaneled walls. Bright orange, navy, and silver helmets—the whole NFL rainbow—were lined up behind the bar above kegs of draft beer. Game films were projected onto white screens at opposite ends of the dining room. The salad bar was fashioned from a red racing car split in half. Crossed hockey sticks indicated the men's room; a bowling pin pointed the way to the powder room. The menu, printed on score cards, listed bar-b-q ribs, burgers and chili. The bartender wore a black-and-white striped referee shirt and blew a silver whistle when he put up a drink order for one of the waitresses, who were outfitted as Dallas Cowboys cheerleaders. Evo ordered two beers from a blond Cowgirl teetering in high white boots and pulled out a chair for me at a table in the corner.

"You didn't miss a trick," I said, eyeing the hockey puck ash tray by the catsup bottle.

"Took years to get it just right," Evo replied with pride. "I've had good offers for this place, but I'm not selling. It'd be like giving away your first kid. Which reminds me. How come your mother didn't tell me she was pregnant?"

"I don't think she felt she knew you well enough. Or maybe she thought you wouldn't believe her."

"I would have taken her word. I'd have married her." Old school honor. Step up and marry the girl. Check.

"I don't think she wanted to get married. She wanted to go to school, write, and travel. You know." The marriage of Bev and Evo was difficult to imagine.

"But I would have taken you if she didn't. She should have told me." Evo thumped the tabletop for emphasis. I was moved by his declaration; he meant it.

What would my life have been like with Evo as a father?

"It turned out okay. I have great parents."

"You got any pictures?"

"Of my folks?

"No, of her. Your mother. Maybe if I see a picture, I'll remember who she is."

"You mean you don't remember her?"

"Nope. Sorry."

"After how I explained it in the letter and everything?" A wave of panic washed over me. I reached for a cigarette.

"You shouldn't smoke those things," said Evo, holding a match for me. "Bad for your wind."

"But you believed that I was your daughter right away."

"Listen, Doll, the way I was in those days I'm surprised I'm not getting a letter every other week." Evo's eyes danced with amusement—and male pride. "And you come across as something special. Sure, I believe you."

I rummaged through my purse and laid out two photos. "This one's from her high school graduation, just a few months before you met. The other one's a group shot from last January when I found Bev in New York."

Evo held up the first photo and shook his head. "Nope. Can't place her." As his gaze shifted to the other photo the smile faded from his face. "Who's the nigger?"

I was shocked at his use of the "N" word and struggled to keep my composure. It was too early to challenge him. I was still seeking his approval.

"That's her boyfriend, Choco. He's a boxer," I said in the vain hope that Choco's athletic prowess would win points with him.

"He the father of the boys?"

"No."

Evo's eyes narrowed to study the photo more closely. "Another nigger was the father, right?"

"Bev's husband was Black," I said evenly. I decided to leave out the information about Randy's father and the other daughter Bev gave away.

"Boy, she really hit the skids, didn't she?" concluded Evo.

I hesitated. Should I defend Bev, and, if so, for what?

"Bev hasn't had it easy," I said finally. "She's taken a lot of hard knocks starting with her parents throwing her out when she was pregnant. But she's not complaining. She's made her way. She's tough and she's smart and I like her."

Evo's eyes moved from the photo and looked me square in the eyes. "Okay,

Doll, I get the message. She must have something for you to feel that way. Fifty per cent of you is from her, and I like what I see, right? Tell you what. Give me her phone number. I'll call her and wish her Happy New Year and tell her we did a good thing making you. Okay?"

"Now?"

"Just give me the number. I'll do it later."

I hesitated before writing down the number. Maybe I should try calling Bev first to warn her. What if Evo got her when she was on speed or drunk? I looked at my blood father and felt the force of his rollicking optimism, his confident masculinity and knew he would do her no harm.

"Sure," I said, scribbling down the number. "You two really do live on different planets, you know. I don't think you have an awful lot in common."

"Except you," said Evo with a grin. "Hey, you're a good kid. I like the way you stick up for your mother. I hope you get to feel the same way about your old man."

"Too early to tell," I teased back. This humor and good will was shared by both my Italian fathers. I could imagine them in the same room, at the same wedding, enjoying the same ball game. Spinning yarns about Evo was not emotionally difficult for me; not like the churning gut and sweaty palms that took over when I related my meeting with Bev. It was clear she was the source of the wound, the soreness that never went away. Years later I realized that I had never written a poem about either father and, while both have popped up in my dreams, they never have with the frequency nor impact that my mothers continue to have in that netherworld. Mine is a female-centric psyche. Just is.

"It's no act. This charm is one hundred per cent natural," he claimed. He opened his arms and shrugged. It is true, I thought. He *is* charming and easy; charismatic without being cunning—and very attractive. His role in my life was a welcome addition, like a free dessert after a restaurant meal. Bev, however, was the main course, the one I consumed to feed a hunger.

The Mini's house was situated in an area on the outskirts of Denver developed in the early sixties. Ranch houses alternated with split levels along quiet streets. Each house had a wide drive and a slender tree on the parkway that was a generation away from providing shade. I spotted the Mini house as soon as we rounded a curve and spied a tan ranch house with a plastic Santa in the yard dressed in a Denver Bronco jersey and helmet. Blinking Christmas lights ringed the picture window and arched over the front door.

Kelly announced that we were to be roommates and led me to her bedroom at the end of the hall. Above the twin bed near the window she had taped a sign written in orange crayon: "Welcome Sister Janine." Balloons and streamers hung off the maple wood bedpost.

"Thanks," I said, giving her a hug. "Only the sign makes me sound like a nun."

With newly found Mini family, Kelley, Evo and Danny, 1975, Denver.

"Oh, I didn't mean *that*!" she giggled. "You're not at all like the nuns at Sacred Heart."

"Well, that's a relief," I said, and then something inside just seemed to collapse and I desperately needed to lose consciousness. Whenever I dove too deeply into my birth family I was tempted to sleep or have a drink; anything to take the edge off my anxiety. "Tell you what. I need to lie down. You can get me up in an hour and we can talk some more, okay?"

"You want to take a *nap*?"

"I know," I said, sympathetically as I pulled off my boots. "I hated naps when I was eleven years old, too. Now they're my salvation."

I swung my feet up onto the bed and was asleep before Kelly had reluctantly pulled the door closed on her way out. An hour later I came out of a deep sleep as something cold and wet repeatedly insisted itself across my face. I opened my eyes to meet the gaze of a large, drooling German shepherd.

"Bronco wants to meet you," Kelly announced. I sat bolt upright and petted Bronco gingerly behind the ears. "Mom wants to know if you want a drink before dinner."

"A Scotch on the rocks would be lovely. More than lovely." I followed Kelly and Bronco down the hall and almost ran into a young man leaning on the counter as I rounded the corner into the kitchen.

"Hi. I'm Danny. Your brother." I turned and stared at him with a jolt of recognition. He was a few inches taller than me with a very familiar jaw line and long light-brown hair. He took a sip from his glass and grinned revealing his dimples. "Yeah, we do look alike, don't we?"

"How does it feel to be the *second* oldest suddenly?" I queried, accepting his brotherly hug.

"Doesn't bother me. I'm still bigger."

We made our way to the living room where Carol joined us carrying a drink tray that she set down on the coffee table. When Evo arrived we moved to the dining room for dinner. As we took our seats, a slender blond teenager slipped into the room and took the chair next to Carol.

"Hey, Chris," Evo called out. "This is your sister, Janine. Aren't you going to say hello?"

"Hello," he barely got out as he stared at his plate.

"Hi, Chris," I said brightly. Another Chris. One half-Black street kid in New York, one mute angel-faced kid in Denver suburbia. Both Chris. Both brothers. I tried to puzzle out the jump of genes: I looked more like Bev than Evo, but most closely resembled Danny. Bone structure from one, coloring from another, a passion for literature from Bev, the Beat; coordination and sports ability from Evo, the Jock/Hero. I whirled through the winding path of the double helix. Within one short year, I had acquired two extra parents, six brothers, and two sisters. Absorbing and sorting through this tangle of relationships would go on the rest of my life.

"Dig in," said Evo. He lifted the cover off the platter of rare filet mignon. I blanched. I had not consumed a piece of red meat in almost two years. It was the era when *Diet for a Small Planet* was in vogue, and I had taken the moral position that the world was hungry because corn grown to feed cattle could be better directed to feed the starving in India. Or maybe it was China. I could imagine the geographic location of the redirected corn quite vividly. I kept my mouth shut and passed my plate to Evo who loaded it up with mashed potatoes, peas, and an immorally large serving of bleeding cow. Danny piled a salad drenched in Thousand Island dressing on my side plate. I somehow got one mouthful after another down while listening to stories about Danny's horses, Evo's tales about the new club, and Kelly's latest achievements in art class. I tried to draw Carol and Chris into the conversation but received only monosyllabic responses. Their position was clearly that of eclipsed moons in the shadow of the massive Jupiterian planet that was inhabited by the brunette faction of the

Minis.

"What's for dessert?" asked Evo, pushing himself away from the table. Kelly jumped up and cleared the plates.

"Your favorite chocolate cake," said Carol. "In honor of the occasion." She gave me a quick smile then stood up to help Kelly clear the table. I tried to help but Carol would not hear of it, which was just as well, since I was having serious problems keeping my dinner down in my outraged stomach.

"Hope you brought some warm clothes," said Evo.

"I've been warm enough so far," I answered. "After all, it's warmer here than in Chicago."

"Not if you're sitting in the grandstand all afternoon in Mile High Stadium." Evo flashed a broad grin and flourished two tickets in the air. "Bronco playoff game tomorrow."

"Wow, where'd you get those?" demanded Kelly.

"Your old man still has connections."

I looked around the table and shook my head. "No, really, Evo. You should take Kelly, or Danny or Chris . . . or Carol."

"I'm bartending at the Half Time tomorrow. I'll see it on the big screen where it's nice and warm," said Danny, lighting an after-dinner Marlboro. Okay, same brand that I smoked.

"It's all right," said Kelly. "I go most of the time and my friend Susie has a birthday party tomorrow."

"Carol and Chris hate football so that leaves us. Make you feel better? Carol can give you some extra clothes to keep you warm. No problem."

"Sure," said Carol. She placed a slab of cake in front of Evo with a glass of milk.

"Eat up," he said. "Got one more place to show you."

"Tonight?" I had been looking forward to collapsing in front of the television to work on my digestion.

"The Corral. It's my country and western place. Real hot right now. You'll like it."

Fifteen minutes later, we were in the station wagon headed across town.

"So, how you like everybody so far?" asked Evo.

"Carol is a sweet woman," I answered slowly. "Kelly is dynamite. Danny's attractive. I can't quite get a line on Chris."

"Quiet type. Like his mother's family. He's okay, though."

"What about the other two boys. Where are they?"

"I never see Doug. My first wife walked out on me when the boys were little and took Doug with her. Never see him at all."

"Sorry." Evo's manner was matter-of-fact, but I could tell that the split bothered him.

"Ah, it could have been worse. I got Danny and Dean. My mother looked after them until I hooked up with Carol."

"And Dean?"

Evo shook his head and slapped the steering wheel with his open palm. "Jesus, that kid's a wild man. I think he's in L.A. He scares me because he's just like I was at his age. Good thing he's not flying B-17's." Evo laughed and looked over at me. "If he lives to twenty-five he'll be one helluva guy." Wild man, indeed. Somehow Evo survived as a bombardier in a B-17 flying thirty-three missions over Germany. The odds were certainly against his survival. There was a name for it; he was a member of The Lucky Bastards Club. That word again, but this time connoting bravery and pride rather than shame.

The fenced in parking lot of the Corral was half-filled. Evo got out of the station wagon and looked over the cars that were parked near the building.

"She's not here yet. Let's wait inside."

"Who's not here?" I asked, thinking for a moment that there was another sister in the mix.

"Laura," said Evo. "My girlfriend."

I stopped dead in my tracks in the middle of the parking lot. It was not an answer I had expected.

"It's not like you think," Evo hurried to explain. "For fifteen years with Carol I never laid a hand on another woman. Then—boom! There's Laura. I'm crazy about her."

"You don't have to explain to me."

"No, no, I want you to understand. You came out here to see who I am, so here's the whole story. Carol and I have hardly slept together the past couple of years. I'm just fifty. I'm not ready to call it quits, you know what I mean? With Laura it's like I'm nineteen again. It's terrific!"

"Okay. So, I'm happy for you."

"I can't leave Carol—I'd lose Kelly and that'd kill me." I wondered at the omission of Chris. "Laura's a widow with a teenage kid. She doesn't want to get married. Everything's fine. Nobody's getting hurt."

I thought of Carol's drawn face, her anxious look as she placed the cake in front of Evo; her comment about there not being enough of him to go around. The plaintive wail of a country singer floated towards us from the club. Complicated sex lives. Yes, I got that. I started to giggle as I headed for the door.

"What's so funny," asked Evo, falling into step beside me.

"Relax. I've got one, too."

"One what?"

"Girlfriend. I've got a girlfriend, too. Her name's Heather. We've been together a year. I'm sure we both feel better now that we've confessed our sexual secrets." I opened the raw plank door to the Corral and stepped into the club before Evo had a chance to respond. A spotlight was focused on a band in the corner playing a John Denver song. The three men and girl singer wore cowboy hats, jeans, and elaborately tooled boots. They were all in their twenties and sang with emotion, if not virtuosity. The knot-studded tables near the band were filled with young people drinking beer and eating pretzels from large red and yellow bowls. Sawdust covered the concrete floor.

"Let's sit over here." Evo steered me to a back table and sat me down to face the band. "Don't you like guys?" he asked as soon as the waitress went back to the bar with our order.

"I like men. I just don't sleep with them anymore," I said, reaching for a cigarette.

"Did you like it when you did? Some guy hurt you, or what?" Evo's face had lost its playful twinkle.

"It was fine. There's no big tragedy to tell. I prefer women. I *like* women better. Or maybe I should say I like men, but I fall in love with women."

"Who's the guy?" Evo's brow was furrowed. "I mean, you're so pretty, is your girlfriend kind of, you know, more like a guy?"

"Not at all. She's shorter than I am and sort of looks like a blond Audrey Hepburn. She wears more eye liner than I do, and higher heels. She's an actress. And like you say, nobody's getting hurt."

"Ouch." A smile played around Evo's sensual mouth. "Get a guy with his own line."

"She got your number already?" A brunette woman leaned over Evo's chair and gave him a kiss on the cheek. I caught a whiff of a floral perfume.

"Hey, Babe. Sit down. This is my daughter, Janine."

"At last. You're all Evo's talked about for weeks. Glad to meet you. I'm Laura Biondi."

"Yes, I know." She wore a lavender silk blouse that set off her violet eyes and dark lashes. Her long nails were lacquered the same deep pink as her lips. The gold earrings and bracelets were showy without being cheap. I figured Laura to be a very fit forty-two; a woman who exercised in leotards and went skiing.

"Your father's some guy, isn't he?" Laura put her hand over Evo's on the table and stroked his wrist. He smiled and a dreamy cloud passed across his eyes. A current shot between them that I had not seen between Evo and Carol. In fact, Evo barely noticed his wife, as if her fairness made her fade into the pastel decor of their home. Laura, on the other hand, caught and reflected light in the room.

"He's a charmer, all right." I gave Evo a nudge.

"Hey, you should talk."

"Just a chip off the old block, I guess."

"Yeah, with a wire crossed."

"She's got your eyes, honey. Be careful." Laura watched us with amusement.

She knows him well, I thought. She watches out for him. She loves him.

"Laura's going to hostess at the new club. What do you think?" asked Evo.

"Perfect," It all made sense. Laura must be the force behind the white piano and crystal ball.

"I used to help in the kitchen at the Half Time when Carol couldn't make it," explained Laura. "Now that my Bobby's older I want to get out and work more."

"Whew—you should see her in some of those new dresses. I'm going to have to come down every night to keep the guys in line."

A flutter of applause marked the end of the set. I sipped my beer and stifled a yawn. It was all catching up with me; the flight, the food, the extended family that included a sexy mistress.

"I better be running along," said Laura with a smile. "Big day tomorrow."

"We'll pick you and Bobby up at noon, okay? We can get some hot dogs at the stadium."

"I'll bring a thermos of hot chocolate," said Laura.

I looked up in surprise.

"Didn't tell you, did he? That's Evo for you. Bobby's been bouncing off walls for weeks about this game. Super Bowl fever, the Orange Crush, the whole bit. I'm glad you're coming. We can ditch them in the stands and go get warm in the lady's lounge." Laura bent down and gave me a hug. "Welcome to the family."

Evo stood up to hold Laura's coat. "I'll walk you to your car."

"You don't have to, honey."

"Naw, I want to. I'll be back in a minute, Janine."

Evo slipped his arm around Laura and eased her out the door. I smoked two cigarettes and listened to the band. Evo reappeared with lipstick on the corner of his mouth. I took a napkin and rubbed away the pink smudge.

"I like her. I understand. Laura would be a hard one to pass up."

"I'm crazy about her." Evo sighed. "I still don't get it about you, though."

I shifted in my chair. "Talk to Laura. She's a woman of the world."

"I just did. She didn't turn a hair. Said her best friend Candy got a divorce to move in with a stewardess. That it happens all the time. I guess I don't understand women anymore."

"We're not all alike, you know," I said dryly. "Just like men. If everyone had the same taste, you wouldn't need menus."

Evo laughed. "You're quick, you are. Probably too smart for your own good. But you're okay even if you are bent. Let's drop the whole thing, okay? Just as long as you don't put the moves on Laura we're fine."

"What if she makes a pass at me?" I laughed to see Evo's confusion. "Ah, the shadow of doubt. It's good for you."

Evo threw some money on the table and helped me on with my coat. The melody of "Rocky Mountain High" followed us into the chilly night air. Rare fillets, football, and forgotten one-night stands, I reflected. Put that alongside the Greenwich Village Beat scene. Welcome into both worlds. From the point of view of my friends in Yesterday's Children, I was a member of our own "Lucky Bastards Club." I had found, met, and been embraced by both of my birth parents. I was now at the place where the adoptee search manual gave out.

Now what?

Heartland

As soon as we crossed the bridge over the Mississippi into Dubuque, Iowa, Bev told me to pull into the first roadside store to get beer. The two martinis she had gulped down on the plane had worn off around Rockford and she needed to sustain her buzz to face Iowa. At the time, a little more than two years from when I had first stood in her St. Mark's Place walkup, I was still incapable of refusing Bev anything. Neither Bev, Chris, nor Randy had a driver's license, so my job was to transport us the five hundred miles from the Chicago airport to Sioux City, Iowa, in the rented Malibu without a relief driver.

The beer helped. Randy sat in back with Bev, sketching in an Egyptian coloring book with his Venus pencils. He carefully filled in each separate feather on Nefertiti's headdress with a contrasting color. At sixteen, he could barely sign his name, let alone read, and was the father of two babies by his girlfriend back home. Chris sat next to me in the front seat with an Iowa map spread open on his lap, which he studied with intent between sips of beer and long drags on a Marlboro, as if he could decode all this flatland better by seeing it in print than looking out the window. Bev hummed in the back seat and rocked back and forth when the radio played something that had a beat. The theme from *Rocky* was popular then and would come on at least once an hour. An occasional burst of laughter would erupt from her smoky lungs as she swayed. What triggered her? Memories of Iowa childhood? A kinetic side effect from the speed she popped every day?

This was an impromptu visit. I got a call the previous week from Bev. "Hello, my dear. I just came into some bread. We're going to Iowa! Pick us up at the airport on Tuesday. I'm flying as Mamie Stover." The alias was lost on me. It was not until ten years later, when I saw the 1956 film *The Revolt of Mamie Stover* starring Jane Russell as an enterprising prostitute who amassed a fortune as a WWII profiteer in Honolulu, that I got the joke. Once again, Bev had a topically appropriate film character to model when called upon to enact a new role.

Choco, Bev's boyfriend, had been thrown into the slammer when he tried to pass heroin cut with soap to a hippie narc. Bev threw three worn coins and opened her copy of the *I Ching*, the ancient Chinese Book of Change that was used for divination, to get instructions on how to respond to this twist of fate and got #24 (*Fu*, Return). The Chinese character had one solid line at the bottom and five broken lines above—the image of Earth over Thunder. The text counseled her not be afraid to turn back from a bad path; that she was to admit error and to follow the example of good people. It was a time to give up bad ways and to return with a goal or destination in mind. Bev interpreted this passage as a directive to go back to Iowa with her assorted brood, a place she had not set foot in for twenty years. And, since Choco had already passed $2,000 worth of soapy coke before he got busted, the oracle had provided financing as well.

We reached Sioux City after nightfall. I guided the car up Bluff Street, pulled over next to a white frame house with a porch light burning, and turned off the ignition. Bev slid out of the back door and made her way up to the porch steps with Chris, Randy, and me, weary beyond words, bringing up the rear. A silhouette of a stooped man was outlined in the screen door.

"It's Bev, ain't it? Just don't stand there. Come on in. You know we don't lock things much around here. And shut that door quick after you. Don't want them bugs buzzing around here all night."

"Hiya, Jake." Bev slipped through the door quickly. We each filed in after her in rapid succession and stood in the living room while Jake eyed each one of us up and down. Bev, the arch hipster, fidgeted girlishly in front of her father, then impulsively threw her arms around him and laid her head against his chest. He closed his arms around her without hesitation and patted her gently on the back while over her shoulder, through his thick glasses, he sized up his three grandchildren. "Come on in and sit yourselves down in the parlor. It's getting all crowded up here in the hall. Want a beer, Bev?" he asked as we settled into the sofa and two chairs in the front room. "I sure could use one."

"Oh, *yes*," swooned Bev. "Love one."

"I'll get it," offered Randy jumping to his feet. "Where's the frig?"

"Through the dining room there in the kitchen. And there's some pop in there for you kids, too."

"Beer's fine," said Randy with a shrug as he sauntered off.

"How old's that kid?" Jake asked Bev.

"Sixteen. Beer won't hurt him."

"Neither would a haircut."

"Neither would a vasectomy," said Chris.

"What's that you say?" asked Jake, turning his good ear towards Chris.

"Never mind," said Bev hastily. "Bad case of sibling rivalry is all."

Randy managed to carry back all five beers at once by dangling the necks between his fingers.

"You don't say much, do you?" Grandpa Jake asked. He sat far back in his reclining chair, peering at me framed between his splayed feet propped on the elevated footrest. "Lord, Bev, she's the image of your mother, don't you think?"

Great Aunt Eva and Grandmother Exzilda Bassett (birthgrandmother), Blue Earth, Minnesota, sometime during World War I.

This was the first I heard of the resemblance. I wanted to see photos. I needed physical proof of my connection to a lineage. I scanned the room and spied a cluster of pictures on one wall in the adjoining dining room and wandered towards them as I gulped my beer. I was searching for family features in the jumble of faces and felt a thrill whenever a nose, the slant of a brow, or a frozen gesture echoed what I saw each day in the mirror.

"Well, I'm pretty tired and I bet you are, too. I'm going to sleep out here. The boys can go upstairs with the borders. I'm going to give you gals my room." Jake heaved himself out of the chair and stood next to me in front of the pictures that obscured the faded floral wallpaper. I felt his hot breath on my neck. We were about the same height, though he must have been taller as a young man.

"Who's this here, Jake? A cousin?" I pointed to the picture of a woman I was drawn to. Surely she was an artist of some sort. Those eyes. That elegant form.

"Her? Oh, she's a daughter-in-law of the second missus, I think. Never did get most of them straight."

"You mean these aren't Phipps family pictures?"

"Naw, they're all her family. Been up long as I can recall. Just didn't make any sense to change them when she passed on. They fill up the wall real nice, don't you think?"

"Yeah, I guess so." I fought back a wave of resentment. How could he be so casual? Why didn't he have photos of his own children and grandchildren on that wall? Didn't it matter to him? And if not, maybe I didn't matter either and the entire journey was pointless.

"You want to see pictures?" he asked, as if reading my mind.

"Of *course*. Why do you think she's here?" blurted out Bev as she walked into the dining room with a fresh beer and sat down at the table. "Do you really think Sioux City's the most sought-after vacation spot in America?"

"Then why *you* here?" he shot back. "You already know what we all look like." Bev laughed nervously and lit a cigarette. During the awkward silence that followed I joined her at the table, lit a companionable Marlboro, and finished my beer. Randy and Chris went out to the car for the bags.

The next day I poured over Jake's collection of family photos, providing a window on my bypassed connection to another life. There was a sepia-toned photo of my grandmother taken around the time of the Great War that made me catch my breath. She must have been in her early twenties—a new bride. Jake had met her the previous year when he was working on a threshing crew in North Dakota. She had been the work party's cook. In the photo her head was bent over as she drank from a hose, her profile sharply etched against the prairie rolling out to the horizon. Jake handed it to me with a shaking hand. Yes, I understood how he saw her reborn in me.

I picked up another photo taken at Christmas 1948 that displayed the entire Phipps family gathered for the holiday. My grandmother's hair was wavy and white. She sat in the front row next to her husband with her three daughters arrayed in chairs on either side. Behind them stood the four boys: Howard, with his square jaw and squinty eyes; Fred, standing at military attention; Johnny, languid and dreamy-eyed; and Danny, straining hard to look older.

"Take a good look," Bev blurted out, waving the hand that held a Gauloise. "That's your first family snapshot. I was three months gone with you in that one. And that was the last time we were ever all together in one room." I looked hard at Bev's midsection concealed in the light tailored suit and tried to discern a bulge that revealed my fetal presence. My aunts and uncles clustered around their parents, one branch destined to become farm wives, mailmen, a California banker, and a career military man. The other Phipps limb was predisposed towards boozy destinies as Las Vegas dealers, habitués of the local drunk tank and my very own genuine Greenwich Village Beat mother.

I moved on to scanning the obituaries of my great-grandfather, a pioneer who had died after being kicked in the head by a mule, and Jake's mother, the maybe Sioux, who lived to the age of ninety-three and died in 1965. I copied all the articles into a journal I had brought for this very purpose, noting the birth dates and deaths: kidney failure, a brain aneurysm, complications from diabetes. With this information I could fill out my own medical records with accurate information for the first time in my life. I had relatives and ancestors, a double helix connection with humanity. At last.

Years later I realized the full significance of the last Phipps family photo. All my life I've had an emotionally fraught time between Thanksgiving and Christmas. In my twenties, I learned not to drink too much during the holidays as I tended to go off the rails. In later years, I would keep celebrations low key and packaged self-care as a Christmas gift to myself. I tried searching childhood memories looking for events during the holidays that would account for "anniversary" anxiety, but only came up with happy rituals and memories with my Veto family. Just typical holiday depression then, I concluded. Or, perhaps, seasonal affective disorder. Another, deeper explanation surfaced while reading about how children of Holocaust survivors are affected in the womb by the trauma of their mothers and can even pass that trauma on to their own children to the third generation. That wordless wound that cannot be articulated. I do not know what pregnant Bev sought from her family when she returned to Iowa for Christmas in 1948, but what she got was rejection and banishment. I was *there* when Bev's own mother threw her out. The mother compact, the primal connection, was broken. Bev absorbed that cruel lesson and five months later, in turn, gave me away. I really do not think she ever recovered.

Later that day Chris and I joined our grandfather in his old brown Ford for a tour of Sioux City en route to the grocery store on the other side of town. Randy decided to stay put and sit in the rental car on the street, cruising for girls who might walk by and think he could drive. Jake pointed out the meat packing plant where he had worked, the red brick high school on the hill in the shape of a medieval fortress that Bev had attended, and the antique shop where my grandmother had worked for a few years in the fifties. He pulled into a vast parking lot with cracked asphalt dotted with sprigs of grass and parked in the far corner away from the entrance, "To avoid crazy drivers," as he put it. It was a large store, midwestern in its extravagant use of space. Chris marveled at its wide aisles and cheap prices comparing it to the cramped, expensive deli near his apartment on East Eighth Street.

Jake led us down the aisles seeming to know exactly what he was after. At one point, in the paper aisle, he paused. "Lord, can you beat that?" He shook his head and held up at arm's length a package of four blue-tinted rolls of toilet tissue. "Eighty-nine cents for asswipes. I have half a mind to go back to using the Sears catalog." He sighed and flung the package into the cart. It was filling up with beef, pork, potatoes, and noodles; a few frozen and canned vegetables; cream, peanut butter, and Velveeta cheese. This artery-clogging diet should have finished him off a decade ago, I mused.

Just as this thought entered my head, an old man ahead of us in the aisle started weaving unsteadily on his feet and fell over onto his back. His jaw dropped open and he began gasping like a smallmouth bass on the bottom of a boat. Jake, who was in the lead, did not break stride. He moved toward his fellow Iowan, and, upon reaching the prone figure, stepped right over him and proceeded to the checkout counter. A middle-aged woman rounded the aisle and fell to her knees by the man before Chris and I could get to him.

"Dad! Daddy!" she repeated over and over. The produce man in a white apron loosened the sick man's collar and belt. Another employee was dispatched to call the emergency ambulance. Chris and I wordlessly exchanged glances and backed down the aisle with the cart in the other direction to join Jake at the checkout counter on the far side of the store.

Twenty-five years later I was reminded of this scene when speaking with my cousin Sue, who lived in Northern California, near where Bev had spent the last two decades of her life. She was reminiscing on how tough Bev had been; how she had survived when those around her had perished. Sue had been the one on the scene after Randy leapt to his death out of Bev's window at the Wong Center, the subsidized assisted living building where Bev had a studio apartment. She had taken Bev to the Denny's restaurant next door after the police had finished questioning her. It was one of the two places to which Bev could walk, trailing her oxygen tank. Anything more than half a block's distance was out of the question. When they had finished their dinner, and were returning to the Wong Center, Sue tried to steer Bev around to the front door of the building to avoid the men who were still hosing down the gory pavement in back where Randy had landed. "No, no," Bev had insisted. "Let's go the back way. It's much shorter." And with that Bev strode over the shiny pavement, splashing rusty pink spots along the side of the oxygen cart she towed behind her.

It was in Iowa, though, that I had my first experience with the Phipps steely will in the face of mortality. Chris and I came up to Jake at the checkout counter and found him standing opposite a cashier who was openly flirting with him as he unloaded the cart. She was in her late 50s with a round face, bottle-coaxed blond hair, and bright coral lipstick that clashed with her red cashier's smock. One shoulder rose higher than the other in a perpetual half shrug.

"These young people yours?" she asked him sweetly. She counted the money he handed her slowly, evening out the wrinkles on each bill and turning all the faces in the same direction.

"Yeah. Grandkids." Jake reached for a grocery bag and started to load the canned goods into the bottom.

"Don't recall seeing you before. Phipps or Kidd?"

"Shelton and Veto," I answered brightly. "New York and Chicago."

"Jake, you never told me about them! How nice! My name's Dolly. How long are you . . ."

Jake swung the last bag into the cart and pushed it out of the checkout onto the rubber mat of the automatic door. I gave Dolly our goodbyes and hurried to catch up with Jake.

"Why'd you ignore her?" I asked him. "She seemed real nice."

"She's been after me to marry her ever since the second missus passed on," snorted Jake.

"Well, is that such a crime?" I asked.

"Too old for me." Jake slammed the trunk.

"Too old? She can't even be sixty!"

"It ain't age. She's all dried up. No juice left in her. I tried. She don't want a marriage, she just wants to be married."

"That's right, Jake," Chris nodded. "Hold out for what you want in women."

"You ever been married?" Jake asked Chris.

"Me? No." Chris blanked at Jake's quick retort.

"Live with a woman?"

"No."

"Then what the hell you know about it?"

Jake got behind the wheel and started up the engine. I slid into the passenger seat. Chris decided to stay in town and get the feel of the place, as he put it, and said he would meet us back at the house later. It is only in retrospect that I realize that he probably went off to shoot up. Years later he called me in New York with a story that his unemployment check did not arrive on time and that he needed fifty dollars, quick, to get something to eat. When he appeared at my door to collect, I offered him part of a pizza that I had just ordered. Sweaty and twitching, he shook his head, and took the fifty dollars with a polite, if hurried, thank you. I did not speak to him again for five years, when he called me from a drug rehab in Florida to make amends as part of his program of recovery.

No one was home when we got back to Bluff Street. The Chevy was still parked by the curb, ashtray full, but there was no sign of Randy. As we carried the groceries to the kitchen, I noticed a half-completed game of solitaire laid out on the dining room table. It was late afternoon. Shadows pooled on the linoleum floor.

I unpacked the canned goods on the counter and was reaching up to open the cabinet doors when I felt Jake come up behind me, his breath catching in short bursts. He locked his arms around mine and pinned me against the counter edge with his whole weight. In my initial shock, I could not respond as I felt his hot breath on my neck and the unmistakable pressure of his erection against my buttocks.

"See, I'm still a man," he said hoarsely. "Come on. Let's lie down." His bedroom, the room he had given over to Bev and me the night before, was just off the kitchen. I struggled to turn away and was surprised by his strength. "Jake, no," I protested weakly, trying to save myself and be polite at the same time, a habit that has taken most of a lifetime to break.

"Jake, what are you doing?" The voice came from behind us, followed by a nervous laugh. "She's your granddaughter." It was Bev.

Jake loosened his grip and took half a step back. I slumped onto the counter.

"She's so much like Exzilda," he said softly, and turned to exit the screen door into the yard.

"Now you know why we all get in sex trouble," said Bev, her laugh nervous as she extended her half full bottle of beer towards me. "Here. Looks like you could use a drink."

The bottle almost slipped through my hand as I downed it gratefully. Bev lit two cigarettes at once and handed one to me. "Ever see *Now, Voyager*?"

"With Bette Davis and what's his name? Sure. On TV." I tried to stay hip despite my wobbly legs.

"Paul Henreid."

"Yeah. The cigarette scene. I get it." I nodded. Okay, we were back at the movies. Movies helped you cope. I smiled crookedly.

"Right." Bev took a long pull on the new beer she got from the frig. "When we finish these, we can move over to the shot and beer joint I found up the street." Bev slammed the refrigerator door. "Fuck it. Just fuck it all to hell."

That night Bev and I bonded in a drunken stupor. At the local bar, beneath a fluorescent Hamm's beer sign, we talked about books and men and sex and how she learned never to be alone with Jake when she was a girl. We drank and talked until we ran out of money and weaved our way back up Bluff Street, guided by the light of a rising full moon. I hesitated as we neared the house and Bev lurched up the stairs in front of me to peer through the screen. "Come on," she waved. "He's asleep in his chair."

We tiptoed through the dim dining room and into the bedroom where I collapsed across the bed and closed my eyes to keep the room from spinning. Bev must have helped me get into a nightgown, because I did not remember a thing until I woke up four or five hours later in a room fetid with stale tobacco and beer. I stumbled from the bed to the bathroom to throw up. When I got back to the bedroom, moonlight was shining through the window across Bev's face on the pillow. Her ravaged features were softer in moonlight and I was filled with tenderness and trepidation. Was I looking at my own older self? How to take the good and leave the frightening things she bequeathed me? I slid back into bed next to her and gently reached out my hand to touch the side of Bev's throat where I could feel her heart beat, and I wondered at the blood we shared and how it had shaped both our destinies.

I almost threw up twice on the way to my Aunt Becky's farm the next day. The severity of my hangovers usually demanded half a day spent horizontal with a cold cloth over my eyes, but Jake was not going to allow such self-indulgence in his house. At seven-thirty he stood over the bed where Bev and I were still asleep and announced that breakfast would be on the table in five minutes as he pulled the quilt off us on his way out the door. Under Bev's tutelage, I was nursing a hair-of-the-dog beer in the back seat to kick start the day.

We turned onto a side road that curved slightly before ending in front of a frame farmhouse. The barn was set back towards a slight rise in the land. A large chicken coop was set between the house and barn. Pieces of farm equipment lay scattered in the field across from the house. We got out of the car through a cloud of ochre dust that settled in tawny halos like dusty lions' manes around our heads.

First down the steps to greet us was a plain woman in her midthirties with close-cropped dark hair and Harlequin glasses. Rebecca Phipps Longwood.

"Good to see you, Bev." Becky leaned over and gave her sister a quick hug. Bev, dressed in her usual black slacks and t-shirt, gave her nervous laugh, and blinked rapidly. "My kids," she explained, waving at the three of us standing next to her in descending birth order.

"Glad to know you." Becky smiled easily. "Mine are all scattered. Kim will be down in a minute. She had to finish a book, she said. Tom and Carrie are doing chores. Zeke's out somewhere, I guess."

As Becky spoke a lean man with the good looks of the Marlboro man emerged from the barn and strolled towards us. An old tan Plymouth pulled up behind Jake's car. A young blond girl emerged from the chicken coop with a bucket of feed. Five cousins poured from the Plymouth. A small boy with wire-rimmed glasses stood up from where he rested against an apple tree and pushed an envelope he had been writing on into his pocket. He shyly thrust it towards me for approval at dinner. It was a poem.

Phipps' and Longwoods from age seven to eighty clogged the yard. A long table was set up in the clearing between the house and the barn across from the chicken coop. macaroni salad, fried chicken, red and green Jell-O molds, rolls, orange Kool-Aid and beer were clustered in the middle with paper plates and plastic cups arrayed around the edges.

A red Dodge glided up the drive, and Bev looked up expectantly. Her beloved brother Bobby, whom she had not seen in twenty-five years, was in the passenger seat. When the car rolled to a stop, Bobby eased out slowly and steadied himself with one hand on the roof of the car. His white hair was combed straight back from his forehead and his skin was stretched tightly across his hollowed features. His blue eyes were unfocused and tentative. The driver was a woman with salt and pepper hair, wearing bifocals, and dressed in dark stretch pants and a print blouse. She, too, moved slowly but with great dignity, her smile subtle and knowing. She reminded me of the picture of Jake's mother and I realized that she must be Sioux as well.

"Here comes trouble," mumbled Jake, his mouth full of macaroni salad. "Drunks. Both of them. They hole up in a little motel outside town and take turns mopping up each other's puke and screaming so's to raise the dead. Worthless, both of them."

A sadness settled over me as I watched Bev tenderly approach the beautiful, broken couple. I was working on a second beer myself to help ease my hangover and was in no position to sit in judgment on anybody's drinking habits. Bobby's ashen face lit up as Bev drew near and I saw the ghost of the handsome man beneath the graying skull. Brother and sister embraced. These were kin of mine. It was the first time I had thought of that word in connection to a group of people, but it seemed right somehow just then. I looked around to the others and made mental note of all the eyeglasses and light complexions and the long strides. Aunt Becky observed my searching glances and asked if I wanted to look at the chickens. We walked over to the coop near where some of the children were playing.

Becky's daughter Kim bounded into the coop and flushed out the chickens for me to admire.

"Some of those little chickens look different," I said to my adolescent cousin.

"They're ducks, that's why," she explained. "Their mother died and the chickens took them in."

"Funny thing about ducks raised by chickens," said Aunt Rebecca slowly as she leaned into the fence. "When the whole bunch get near water for the first time, the ducklings jump right in and start to swim. Makes the mother hen crazy. She thinks they're going to drown and she clucks at them from shore. Thing is, they're still ducks, don't you know."

I looked at my aunt, who was only eight years my senior, and tried to figure out if this was just a casual comment or she was trying to tell me something.

"Thank you," I said softly and hesitated. "We've spoken before, you know. I called you pretending I was a paralegal to get information about Bev. Sorry for the charade."

"I know. I remember."

"Of course. You figured that out."

"I mean I knew then," said Rebecca. "Right when you called. I knew it must be you."

"Then thank you again, from the bottom of my heart," I said. "Without the information you gave me, I might not have been able to find Bev."

"Enough time had gone by. It couldn't hurt anything or anyone anymore. Besides, you had the right."

"I did?" I flushed. I still had trouble believing I was entitled to know about my own beginnings.

"Sure. Sure, you do. Look, if you have any questions about the family or anything, just ask me. Or write me later. I'm what you'd call the unofficial family historian. I know as much as anyone, I guess. I have Grandma Exzilda's Bible, some of Grandpa John's old harnesses in the barn—all that sort of stuff."

I was invited to the family reunion in the late '90s but didn't go due to work demands. Aunt Rebecca and I had lunch in New York when she was visiting with a group of friends for a few days, and I did return to Sioux City, in 2015 when I was working on this manuscript.

I have kept in touch with Rebecca's daughter, Kim, who not only looks the most like Bev of any of my cousins, but is also most like her in life choices, sans the debilitating alcohol and drug habit. She, like her Aunt Bev, attended the University of Iowa. After graduating she served in the Peace Corps in Thailand, moved to Germany, then Holland. Once back in the United States with her biracial daughter, she returned to school for an MBA, had a son and worked in finance for PBS. After acquiring a husband and another child she moved the entire tribe to Hawaii to take a job there. In recent years she started a yarn shop business but is seriously considering returning to the Midwest. Kim is kin. This is what most people have: people who look like them and have similar interests and talents within their extended family. I venture to guess that most people take this identity-anchoring phenomenon for granted. I never do.

That afternoon in Sioux City, the Phipps clan ate and strolled across the fields and took turns riding half-broken horses over the gently sloping land. The cousins took pictures of each other and us in varying groups sitting on the tractor, inside the hay wagon, against the endless blue sky. I started a Phipps family album from that trip and added to it over the years with snapshots I received from Becky in Christmas cards, or ones of Randy and Chris and Bev after one of our infrequent meetings over the next twenty years.

For the rest of Bev's life we exchanged occasional letters, Christmas cards and phone calls. On average, we spoke a few times a year; calls that were comforting and unnerving by turn. One time, having not spoken for a half year, Bev answered saying she almost did not pick up because she was immersed in re-reading *Anna Karenina*. And, sitting on my desk in front of me, was my own copy of *Anna Karenina* that I just happened to be re-reading myself.

I keep two separate family photo albums, in respect for my mother, who never wanted to meet or to know too much about Bev. I imagine that Marie Walton Veto would be offended to have her own image within the same bindings as the stranger who had given birth to me. I never labored under the impression that I was to reconcile these women to each other in life; only to modulate their vastly different voices within my own psyche. Through the years I gradually integrated my dual maternal heritage and could say "Oh, my mother has small hands," or "A literary bent runs in our family," or "My mother was the most organized person I ever met," and not feel compelled to explain which mother's traits found an echo in me.

I do, however, take pleasure in those moments when the two mothers exist in harmony. During my Manhattan years I attended a production of Martha Clarke's "Vienna Lusthaus," a dream-like dance/theater piece set in *fin de siecle* Vienna, the time of my mother's birth. It was peppered with naked bodies in the throes of a rich pattern of desire, in counterpoint to the costume and custom of formality, a display of Freudian sexuality and nascent militarism. The theater was in the East Village, only blocks from where I had found Bev in 1976. Once a dangerous and derelict neighborhood, it was now the center of the hip, cutting-edge scene. I smiled to myself, taking comfort in the fact that within me the two quite different women had made their jigsaw peace.

If we are lucky, we do make peace with our mothers, living or dead. Bev had her moment when we were driving back to her father's house after the gathering at the Longwood farm. Chris was in the front seat with Jake while Bev and I sat in back. Randy had stayed on at the farm and would be brought home by an uncle. Bev had a beer buzz on and was humming "Take the A Train" as we zigzagged along Military Road and Talbot, across the fields toward the city. At the top of a rise Jake took a left turn between two stone gateposts under a wrought iron arch that spelled out "Mt. Calvary Cemetery." Bev caught on immediately and lurched forward between Jake and Chris.

"Oh, no you don't. You're not going to parade me in front of her grave for your family day finale. Let me out of here."

In response, Jake slammed on the brakes, propelling us forward with a nasty snap that loosened Bev's grip on the door handle. He spun around and fixed Bev with a thunderous gaze.

"You're a growed woman and I don't say nothing about your life, or where you been for twenty years, or how come you didn't come back when we put your mother in the ground. You were so busy fighting with her you couldn't see how alike you were, with your pride and set ways. I want to show these children of yours where we laid their grandmother. And if you can't show respect for her, think of them and keep your goddamn smart mouth shut."

And with that, Grandpa Jake turned around with surprising speed for a man of eighty and with perfect control guided the car through the gates at a respectful ten mph. Bev slumped into the back corner. I reached over to squeeze her limp hand, while Chris stared out the passenger window at the granite and bronze rectangles on the ground marked by crosses, withered bouquets, or the frozen, open armed embrace of the Virgin. An air of neglect hung over the place. The grass was sparse; the earth marked with gullies that ran in vertical, twisted patterns down the eroded hillside. The road wound counterclockwise around a hill and came to a stop near a small sign stuck into the ground with the word, "Golgotha" stenciled on it in black letters. Bev popped open a new can of beer she drew from her bag and downed half of it in one gulp.

"Come on, let's get this over with," she mumbled.

We followed Jake around to the west side of the hill. No crosses or stones rose from the side of Golgotha. Bronze headstones surrounded by dry scrub grass marked the graves. Jake stopped abruptly, folded his hands in front of his stomach, and cast his eyes downward to the plate inscribed "Phipps" across its width with his first name and birth date on the left side. The right half of the headstone was filled in with "Exzilda Phipps, Born May 30, 1896. Died May 15, 1963."

Chris glanced at the grave, then walked down the slope to study the fading light on the fields. He seemed to feel no sense of loss about this grandmother. His memory of her went back to the age of three when he lived with her for a while when Bev was attending the University of Iowa. He remembered her stern face and the disapproving looks that even then he knew had to do with his being fathered by a Black man. But mostly he remembered the pain when she tried to remove this "blackness" from his foot with an emery board after his bath, as if the soap and water alone weren't enough to bring his mocha complexion up to an acceptable level of whiteness.

The half-empty can of beer slipped from Bev's hand. It bounced off the corner of the headstone with a metallic clang and rolled down the hill, anointing other graves. She let out a groan and sank to her knees beside her mother's gravestone. At close range she could see the dried mud caked inside the raised letters and numbers. She picked at the mud clogging the *E*, the loops of the *8*, the circle within a *P* with a broken fingernail, and tried to brush the crumbs of dirt off the headstone into the grass.

Jake turned away and retreated a short distance around the hill. I didn't know whether to follow him and leave Bev alone or to remain in mute support.

"I didn't think it would hit me like this. I didn't think I cared," Bev croaked. She was stunned by the fact that she *did* care and could cry for the mother who would not or could not care for her or protect her when she had needed her so desperately.

Our mothers. Drunks, abandoners, idols, nurturers, abusers; our doubles or mirror images, dwelling on Iowa plains or the Vienna Woods, but always, always deep within us.

Whatever the configuration, how can we *not* care?

I was still very much a daughter, responsible only for myself, preoccupied with knitting together strands of my heritage, parsing nature vs. nurture, charting a career, exploring romance: it was all about me. Although there were four adopted children in my Veto family, I was the only one ever to launch a search. My brother Bob and cousins Dennis and Cindy started families of their own in their teens or early twenties. They were parents who kept their children, born before or after marriage. It is as if their primal drive were to create a human with their genetic material as soon as possible; to connect with similarities and traits like their own; to start another lineage early since they had lost theirs at birth. At that time, I did not feel the urge for motherhood myself. Instead, my quest during my twenties was to move back in time for connection rather than forward into creating a new tribe.

Another force was working in me below the surface as I matured, however, until a powerful urge for motherhood surfaced more than a decade later in a different city. This eruption was entwined with the descent of *Colpo di fulmine*, as the Italians call it. The thunderbolt. The thunderbolt is a force of blissful chaos. It cracks open your chest and spills out your soul. Once the thunderbolt hits, your life is irrevocably changed. Ava flashed into my life the summer of 1990, igniting inexplicable passions and positing new constellations of family.

Generation

At a Poets and Writers benefit at The Carlyle, New York, 1983.
Photo courtesy of Nancy Crampton.

My Turn(ing)

I saw myself as more of an Auntie Mame than a mother; more a lover than a matriarch; more suited for a romantic dyad than the family circle. This self-image held throughout the opening months of my dizzying affair with the glamourous and enigmatic Ava. We met in the heat of the summer of 1990 when her nine-year-old daughter Elizabeth was away at camp and the live-in housekeeper was in Hungary visiting family. We were free to be with each other in her empty Park Avenue apartment, her place in Connecticut, my Sag Harbor cottage or funky walk-up crash pad in SoHo. We walked country roads and beaches, dined, attended concerts, and strolled through galleries cocooned in our very own Summer of Love.

One late summer morning in Sag Harbor I woke and turned over to behold Ava beside me. It was like waking from a dream into a dream-like reality that was too good to be true. I slipped out of bed, eased over to the wooden chest that served as a window seat in my bedroom and stared at the miracle of Ava in my bed, her riot of wavy hair spread over the pillow case framed by the pale rose design of the sheets. After Ava left me, I could not bear to sleep on those sheets for three years. I could not put them on my bed without seeing Ava and tear up in anguish. But that morning the sun found a path through the blinds and dappled her with light. My heart expanded in my chest with a wave of gratitude. I thanked whatever force animated the universe for this soul-melding ecstasy. I promised I would remain grateful whether it lasted a week, a year, or the rest of my life. I promised.

Our easily arranged time together ceased once Elizabeth and the housekeeper returned to New York and I became the "friend" rather than lover. At first, I chaffed at the restriction but grew to enjoy and celebrate the domesticity. I fell in love all over again, my expanding heart encompassing Elizabeth and a shared life within a family of people I loved. And perhaps another child?

I was amazed at the awakening within me to the primal urge of wanting to have a child from my own body. It was as if I suddenly "got" what propelled the human race. For forty years I had been suppressing this urge to have my own child. I thought anew about the reasons my brother Bob married at twenty-one and had three children before he was thirty. He surrounded himself with people who looked like him and kept them close, even employing two of them in his own business. My reticence to see all this up until now was a loyalty, of sorts, to my own mother who could not conceive. It was also a way to bolster my own ego so that I never had to directly confront the fact that I was a second choice; the fallback position in the Veto's efforts to create a family.

This notion of having a child grew slowly but insistently during my first two years with Ava until finally I knew. I wanted it all. Fairy tales tell about the dangers of escalating wishes when a mere mortal receives extraordinary presents and is emboldened to ask for more. Yes, dear reader, I got greedy. I wanted both the passion of Ava and the comforts of family all rolled into one. And I could not have picked a more impossible person with whom to attempt this slippery trick than the very person who had ignited within me such aspirations.

The time would come when I faced a cruel choice: preserve my connection to Ava or start a family of my own. Only my search for Beverly rivaled the struggle I faced at that crossroads. And once again, the choice was made by forces beyond my control. I learned to live forward, scarred but enriched, enduring loss for a greater healing, and resting in gratitude for outcomes I could not foresee.

Annunciation

It was a Wednesday, six thirty in the evening. Ava was in town. Therefore, I was at the Korda dining room table. Edith, the housekeeper, was in the process of clearing the serving plates of chicken paprikash. Ava sat at the head of the table with Elizabeth at the side and me at the foot. Opposite Elizabeth, a large, very blue abstract painting took up most of the wall furnishing a purposeful contrast to the more traditional elegance of the rest of the Park Avenue apartment. It was four long miles uptown and almost fifteen years since my reunion with Bev. I believed I had made peace with my past. I had a new focus in my life and it was here in this well-appointed apartment, here with this shimmering woman, this heavenly body around which I orbited.

Ava stood up to refill our glasses with Perrier. As she bent over, the subtle fragrance of sandalwood filled my nostrils totally obliterating the aroma of the savory morsels of chicken still on my plate. The scent of sandalwood is forever linked with making love with Ava in my mind. It was always such sweet torture: she was leaning over me but could not be touched.

"Yes, please." Was Ava aware of the effect she had on me? Probably. She had mastered the art of parlaying scarcity into high demand—in the juice business, diplomacy, and erotic management. As one of the few women food brokers on the international scene, Ava had learned to use all her intelligence, family connections, and charm to make her income match her sense of style.

"Mother, may I be excused to do my homework?" asked Elizabeth, scooping up the last four strips of raw red pepper from her plate.

"Yes, darling," nodded her mother.

"I'll be there in fifteen minutes for the math," I said. At the sixth-grade level I could still be of assistance. In another year or two I would have to retreat from the math tutoring and stick with literature and history.

"Great. Mom does it *backwards*."

"Of course," shrugged Ava as Elizabeth skipped around the corner of the table into the hall, narrowly missing a collision with Edith. "If I even dare to suggest that Americans do long division in a totally illogical fashion, she flies into a patriotic rage. Come. Let's sit by the fire. Edith can bring us our tea."

I settled into the chintz-covered love seat by the fireplace as Ava took her place on the opposite, identical loveseat.

"I'm going to Argentina on Tuesday. Some trouble with shipping the apple concentrate."

I still experienced a slight jolt every time Ava announced these intercontinental jaunts with the casualness that other people in my acquaintance rattled off subway stops on the IRT. I still had, and would *always* have, an anxious reaction when someone I loved would suddenly disappear; a residue of adoption abandonment that I learned to identify and tame but never to eliminate.

"Ah," I responded, sipping my South American digestive tea brewed from a plant that did not grow north of the Equator.

"I'm bringing Enrico. You know." Ava smiled and waved her hand. Ever the pragmatist, Ava usually brought along her second in command on trips to South America. While she was unquestionably in control, she had Enrico speak in meetings to preserve the illusion of Latin macho dominance.

"And Elizabeth? Do you want me to watch her for the weekend, or whatever?"

"No, no, thank you, darling. I spoke with Tom. We're switching weekends so she'll be with us this coming weekend instead and go with Tom the following weekend. But thank you. Sorry if this changes our plans, darling, but we'll go away together when I get back, all right?"

Once again, I was rapidly readjusting. Being with Ava was good training in enforced flexibility. Let's see. This meant that the longed-for private weekend of long walks, afternoon siestas in each other's arms followed by languid dinners and back to bed to sleep together through the night, was off. I would be stationed in the guest suite in Connecticut up a separate staircase on the other side of the house. I made a rapid mental shift from anticipation of lust fulfilled to family board games by the fire.

Yes, we would be able to take walks together and Edith would be there, too, so the meals would be prepared for us. Physical contact, however, would be limited to a quick half-hour on the chaise in the pool house on Saturday after dinner before retiring. If I was lucky. And the following weekend, I would be on my own, without either mother or daughter. And then, the following week, I would be in Los Angeles for several days for the ballet. I was the development director of the Joffrey Ballet when it was still based both in New York and Los

Angeles, which bestowed upon me my own familiarity with airports.

"Of course, ah, do you think you'd have some more time before you leave?"

"We have tomorrow night, darling."

"*La Rondine*, of course."

It was Ava's favorite opera; soaring arias and a story line of impossible love. In the bourgeois world of Vienna (Park Avenue?), the lovers could briefly and blissfully co-habit by the sea (vacations?), but not marry. The parallels to our own complicated scenario was uncomfortably familiar. I had picked up tickets as a surprise for Ava several months before. We had fallen into the rhythm of either going out or retiring to my apartment to make love on Tuesdays and Thursdays when Tom would faithfully come to the apartment to have dinner with Elizabeth. Not that Ava ever acknowledged to Tom—or people of her circle at all, really—that she and I were anything other than friends.

"Well, better get on with the math before lights out." I cradled my teacup in the crook of my palm and joined Elizabeth at her desk. "Okay, hon, better take your socks off. We're going to need all our fingers and toes to figure this one out."

Together we puzzled out the mysteries of dividing big numbers by little ones, American style. Physically, Elizabeth was her father's daughter; long limbed, with hazel eyes and chestnut-hair. These and other distinctions of temperament made it easier for me to discern that this was a separate and strong love, not merely an extension of my besotted passion for Ava. Three years of homework, reading bedtime stories, and playing clumsy soccer on the vast lawn of the Connecticut house had awakened a longing for my own child.

I can trace the beginning of my maternal urges to a moment during our first year as a clandestine couple. Ava, Elizabeth, and I were attending a holiday open house at a historic home in New York which was owned by a client of mine. While Ava was off refreshing her drink, I took Elizabeth to a second-floor bedroom to show her the old dresses, jewelry, hats, and shoes I thought she might like. A board member of the old house approached us, smiling, and said "Oh, what a lovely daughter you have, Ms. Veto." An arrow shot through my chest. Ah, if only it were so, I remember thinking at the time. I also experienced a twinge of sadness as Elizabeth shook her head vehemently and said, "No, she's not my mother. My mother is downstairs."

But I would *love* to be your mother, too! a voice deep inside me cried. Even that early into the relationship, I knew that nothing would have made me happier that to create a home with both Ava and Elizabeth. But Ava made it clear that Elizabeth did not need a third parent and she did not have a history of cohabiting with other women, even if they provided the deep connections in her life. I continued playing the Auntie role, bringing back souvenirs from my travels, searching for another sculpted soap animal to add to the collection Elizabeth was amassing in the medicine cabinet of her bathroom.

Edith and Ava appeared at the door, one with an apple cut into eighths and a cup of tea for a bedtime snack, the other with the dog leash.

"Come, I'll walk you halfway back."

I tucked Elizabeth in, kissed her and joined Ava in the foyer.

"Come out of your bunker, Kaiser Wilhelm," commanded Ava in her amused manner. The sprightly dachshund liked to take naps in the nether reaches of the deep hall closet behind the neatly gradated rows of minks, long cloth, and shorter sporty coats. However, when a walk was offered, he wiggled out willingly and offered his neck for the leash.

Once in the elevator we took advantage of the twelve floors of descent for our one kiss and full embrace of the evening. I had learned how to give in to total swoon and to recover in time to resume a placid if somewhat dazed expression by the time the highly polished brass of the elevator doors rolled back on their well-greased track. Ava stepped out with her regal yet languid step (how *did* she do that?) eyes straight ahead past the uniformed doorman who nodded his head in deference as he held the door for Ava and Wilhelm. And, two steps behind, I followed, nodding, and smiling to Joe, who smiled back in a friendly fashion. I was aware that my exchange with Joe revealed me to occupy a lower-class status than Ava who had been raised with servants and more clearly delineated lines of social demarcation.

"You know, the strangest thing has been happening the past several months," I said as we rounded the corner onto 84th Street. Ava cocked her head. "This voice from somewhere inside me, and even some dreams, keeps suggesting that I should have a child. This has been bubbling under the surface for quite a while now, but it's really becoming insistent. Am I going crazy or what?"

"No, darling, this is very normal. Hormones. It happens around forty. Maybe you should consider it. You know, maybe it would be easier if you had a child, too. I think sometimes you don't understand, even though you think you do."

I was about to respond but decided to hold my silence. Whenever I pressed her to integrate our lives more fully, she would bring up Elizabeth as the reason that it would not be possible. That, or sometimes the reason was pressure at work, or the demands of her parents. I long suspected that this kaleidoscope of rebuffs were ploys to protect, instead, Ava's unwillingness to acknowledge our relationship publicly or to make a commitment.

"It's such a new idea for me," I mused. "And yet the urge is so strong ... at least intermittently. I love our time together that feels so familial, and the idea of a child of my own, well ..."

"You must figure out your scenario and then get organized. That's how you do it." Ava paused for Kaiser Wilhelm to lift his leg against the mailbox.

I waited to see if a more personal reaction would follow. "So, you wouldn't mind a baby....?" I finally ventured.

"No, no, it would be wonderful. Elizabeth is so big already. It goes so fast. And maybe it would be good for her, too, to have a little one around." A nuclear reaction went off in my chest. A child of my own and Ava thought it was a good idea! The lid on a long simmering pot blew off. I *wanted* a child and here was a green light from Ava that said it would not cost me her love to follow my heart. This is what it must have felt like to my mother Marie when no child appeared after ten years of marriage and she forged an atypical path to motherhood. I had not felt this kind of call to action, to a quest, really, since I had set out to find Bev.

We reached the corner of Lexington and waited by the pizza parlor for the light to change. Across the street the children's shoe store was featuring ankle-length boots for tots alongside the standard Upper East Side patent leather Mary Janes. I smiled. *A little one around?* Did that mean in the same household or down the street at my studio apartment? Yes, my apartment, to which I had moved from my place in SoHo eighteen months before as a temporary base, to be near Ava and Elizabeth before we created a household together. During the past year Ava had veered in and out of scenarios about how we would do it. Redecorate the study for a bedroom for me? Sell the apartment and move into a large rental together? We had gotten to the point of viewing several apartments just off Park Avenue, but all the three-bedrooms we were shown were a decided comedown from the classic six Ava now enjoyed. Nothing more had been said on the topic for several months. Without realizing it, I was regressing into my role as the outsider child waiting to be asked into the home and family of an already established family.

"Now the father..." I mused out loud. "There's always the old boyfriend route, but I've heard very scary stories about guys changing their minds about their 'noninvolvement' once the child is born or reaches the age when they can play baseball. And sperm donation from gay guys, well, that's out of the question these days. Oh, Ava, if only cloning were more advanced, I'd take a few cells from behind your perfect ears and incubate them."

"Thank you darling," Ava smiled. "Think we'd make a cutie?"

"Oh, indeed. And hardly dim-witted. We couldn't go wrong." I sighed. What a heady thought; a child, a physical child made of the stuff of the woman you loved. I used to downplay this urge to manifest the love two people had for each other as needing to have a child of their own co-joined genes. It was a reflective defense on behalf of my adoptive community. Yet with Ava, I thoroughly got it why the human race continued to reproduce itself this way, despite the atrocities and horrors humans continued to inflict upon one another. "Too bad your brother isn't still alive."

Ava tugged gently on Wilhelm's leash and waved her free hand with her dismissive gesture. "Ach, don't even think it. He wouldn't have made the donation, my dear." Her younger brother, an architect in Buenos Aires, had died of AIDS the year before I met Ava. Yet, in the Korda family code, no one spoke of his gayness or of Ava's for that matter. It was difficult for me to know if all these discrete silences were signs of familial pathology (American interpretation) or merely a different culture and class norm.

When we reached Third Avenue, Ava reigned in the Kaiser and leaned her cheek towards me for our public good-night kiss. Some evenings she would walk me as far as Second Avenue, but tonight was not one of them. I instructed myself not to read too much into this.

"Pretty dreams, darling," she said. "Maybe tonight some answers will come to you."

"You think it comes that fast?" I said, leaning towards her halo of blond, wavy hair and into the fragrant zone of sandalwood to place my chaste kiss on her proffered cheek.

As I walked the remaining blocks to my apartment, I reviewed the catalog of recent Ava "firsts" that indicated we were growing closer to operating like a family unit that could include a child of my own. We had just spent the Christmas and New Year holiday with Ava's parents in Punta del Este. We delighted at our good luck that the German ambassador, who had elected to extend his visit at the Kordas, occupied the guestroom that was supposed to be mine. We were able to share Ava's bedroom for nights of eucalyptus-scented love and lazy afternoon siestas. I played Old Maid and tennis with Elizabeth. Ava and I took time alone together in Buenos Aires to explore a tango bar, eat steak and go home together to her apartment in the fashionable Palermo part of town. Back in Uruguay we all swam together in the pool. Ava and Elizabeth teased me about my feeble attempts at Spanish thank-you's to the fleet of three maids, grounds crew, and caretaker's family. I could not wait until my baby arrived and all *four* of us could visit my parents in Villa Park or even up North so that the kids could enjoy the lake. Even if Ava were traveling, I could take the children. It was probably the happiest holiday of my life. Having a baby was my joyous New Year's resolution.

Was I delusional? As I reflect on that time, I can testify that the boundaries of Ava's strictly compartmentalized life were blurring, one by one. She, too, had become emboldened by love to imagine a shared life. "Ach, if I can't do it with you, I give up," she asserted. She even came to a shared session with Donna, my therapist, and allowed herself to go to another therapist Donna had suggested for a few sessions of her own. Then she called a halt to therapy. "Enough. Jessica is an intelligent woman. I understand what she is getting at. But no more. She wanted me to commit to coming every week, and darling; you know how impossible that is with my schedule. Anyway, I think time at a spa would do me just as much good." She smiled then, her most seductive smile, and I let the topic drop.

Meanwhile, I kept silent about sobering warnings from my own therapist. "It will take years for Ava to commit, if ever," Donna told me bluntly after stating how she liked Ava and understood what attracted me to her. "And she will always be ambivalent. You couldn't have picked a better candidate to rip off the scab on every wound you have if you had planned it." Donna meant my own adoption, of course, and the core issue of abandonment that for others was a metaphor and for me would forever be the psyche-destroying landmine at my core. I remembered vividly how debilitated I had been in my early twenties when Captain Jens disappeared. I also experienced a depression when a woman I had been seeing for a little over a year in my late thirties started sleeping with other women and ultimately dumped me. I was a wreck even after my years of therapy and the fact that I really was not in love with her or thought all that highly of her as an overall human being. Boy, if I had strong reactions to that breakup, what potential powder keg was I playing with now?

And yet, perhaps abandonment was the true bond, the shadow source of the deep connection that did lie between us. Ava's story had the sweep of a David Lean movie epic. She was born in Budapest one year after her parents were reunited, following their release from Auschwitz and a labor camp. The family moved to Germany, of all places, during her early years, then back to Budapest before the 1956 Russian invasion made them flee, once again, to Argentina when she was ten. There she was enrolled in the German school where the tall blond family was assumed to be German Christians. None of the places Ava was raised in were particularly welcoming to Jews.

I heaved an audible sigh as I inserted my key into one of the two outside doors of my apartment building.

And I was surprised that Ava had trust issues, as we naïve Americans say? Nowhere in her history, I now understood, was there a time when it was safe for her to be known. Powerful connections, quick intelligence, and portable assets were the holy trinity of the Korda tribe. And I thought the love of a good midwestern gal would settle her down? In the late twentieth century Western world, the Holocaust trumps all.

***

The very next day I euphorically started researching fertility specialists in New York. Once I shift into quest mode, I tend to hyper focus on details and move through checklists with disciplined speed (a nod of acknowledgement to my executive secretary mother, Marie Walton Veto). It was not unlike my campaign to find Bev fifteen years earlier, but this time I was tracking down a future child instead of a lost mother.

I soon zeroed in on the highly regarded Dr. Varga at nearby New York Hospital and arranged for a consultation. Tall, lean, and dignified, he reached out to shake my hand. "Ms. Veto, a pleasure to meet you. Let's see what we can do for you, yes?" Astonished, I took a seat beside his desk. It did not occur to me until that moment that Varga was a Hungarian name. His accent made him sound like Ava with bronchitis. Surely this was a sign, I told myself, a good omen. A countryman of Ava's would oversee the creation of my child. Perfect. I was far down the path of this story line before I could redirect my attention to the doctor's assessment. While my age was a deterrent, my excellent health (and his great expertise, he managed to imply) prompted him to be cautiously optimistic about my chances to conceive. He had had success with other ladies in their early forties and had the snapshots of happy mature mothers with their babies to prove it.

I joyously gathered up all the reading material he offered and headed home. I could hardly wait to give Ava the update during our nightly good-night phone conversation.

"And would you believe it?" I said at 8:45, not capable of holding off until our usual 9:00 p.m. time. "He uses a sperm bank in Los Angeles and I'm already booked to be there next week for the ballet. I'm going to make an appointment to visit and check it out. Just one more happy coincidence smoothing the way, don't you think?"

"It's all very exciting, darling," offered Ava. "But you must be realistic. I worry about your age and health, although Dr. Varga sounds like an intelligent man. Just sleep on it. And have pretty dreams, my love," she crooned with her signature farewell phrase before we hung up and drifted off to sleep in our separate beds, five blocks and ten floors apart.

I dashed over to the clinic during the two-hour window of time I had before I was to meet the staff at the Music Center to work out the logistics of using the VIP lounge for a pre-performance donor reception on gala night for the ballet's *Nutcracker Suite* engagement. *Nutcracker* in the spring. Guess it went with the palm trees. And since it *was* LA and not New York, it also involved complicated security for the millions of dollars' worth of jewelry that would be "casually" on display and for purchase with a small token percent earmarked for the ballet.

Typically, I would have taken a nap and luxuriated in the quiet time to alleviate the strain of cross-country flights and desperate strategic meetings with board members upon arrival to plot ways of erasing the ballet's mostly self-inflicted deficits. But now with the higher purpose of motherhood on my mind there was no question of sleep. I gripped the wheel of the rented car (since no one took cabs in LA) and sped as fast as I dared to the low, white shoebox of a building that housed the lab plunked down in neither the best nor worst section of the grubby ring around downtown LA. At least there was easy street parking, which left me plenty of time to get acquainted with my child's father. I did not have Bev's option of sizing up Evo sitting next to her at a bar, reacting to his phenomes before going horizontal to produce a child.

An amiable receptionist led me through a honeycomb of cubicles to a side office where another toned, fresh-faced California girl rose to greet me.

"Hi! I'm Ginny. Now, tell me, what kind of guy are you looking for?"

"Ah, healthy, intelligent," I stammered as I eased into the chair facing the desk in the small office. So much for foreplay.

"No, no, this is the time you get to choose. What's your fantasy? Blond? Athletic? A super scientist? A musician? Here, I'll show you. Let your imagination go wild." Ah, California. And what a contrast to the prim administrative efficiency of Miss MacFarland at Chicago's Catholic Charities in the 1970s. It seems gatekeepers of sperm are more welcoming to prospective mothers than adoption guards are to adult children looking for mothers.

Ginny produced a legal-sized sheet of paper from her drawer that listed thirty-five different candidates, all coded by number. The columns by each number listed race, ancestors' origin, height, weight, body build, skin tone, eye color, hair color, blood type, years of college, and occupation. "Just check this out and for the ones that look interesting, I can pull a fuller bio, okay?"

I scanned the list and ticked off numbers into two mental buckets. Bucket One contained candidates that had a physical/ethnic resemblance to me: fair, English/French/Italian/German heritage. The clone bucket. Bucket Two had the "interesting" candidates: the musician, a Mr. Outdoorsman, a Jewish doctor in a nod to Ava's input and a stereotypical assumption of brains. I handed my list with the top six greatest hits circled back to the beaming Ginny, the Valley Girl Sperm Santa.

"Oh, wait a minute. I forgot to tell you. The doctor isn't available. A Jewish lady in New York has cornered his sperm for at least six months."

"I didn't realize that there was a future's market in sperm," I said. "Okay, just throw in Number 62 to round out the half dozen."

The more complete dossiers contained the most amazing information. Precise family histories going back two generations on both sides, giving the number of male and female offspring born to help calculate the likelihood a boy or girl; what each family member succumbed to and at what age; talents and interests one might hope or dread would thread through the genes—piano playing, an attraction to extreme sports, a philosophical bent. Ginny offered the take on who was good looking and who seemed "to have their shit together."

"You know these guys, don't you?" I asked.

"Yes. And for you, I think Number 54 would be great. You look like you could be a couple."

"Yes, if I wanted to play the Marshallian to his Rosenkavalier." That was a throwaway line on Ginny. And since I *was* in LA and not New York, I should have said Mrs. Robinson, instead. But I got some other nugget of information from her that might prove useful in the future—most of this pool had been or were currently affiliated with University of Southern California. And since I had their ages, field of study, and family profile, I also knew that there was a good chance that one day in the future I could help my son/daughter trace his/her own heritage. As a *bono fide* pioneer of the adoptee search movement in the pre-internet 1970s, I knew I had an excellent chance of tracing him, should the time come around for my child. I knew in my bones how this need cries out, especially during adolescence when we try to figure out who we are on so many levels at once.

Over the next two weeks Ava and I narrowed the field down to three candidates. Number 46 was a six-foot, 160-pound teacher of Italian and German heritage. With his olive skin and hazel eyes, he sounded like he could be one of the Veto clan. Ginny told me he was good humored, pleasant, and even-tempered. And since she was a Valley Girl, she also said he had a square jaw and emphasized his ability to tan well and rock climb. The downside for me was the fact that cancer claimed grandparents on both sides of his family and while he had "fathered" in the program, he had an erratic sperm count. At my age, I could not gamble on a hit or miss guy.

Another contender was Number 54, the one Ginny had heavily promoted to me. He was six foot three inches tall, with blue eyes and wavy dark blond hair, of German and English descent. She claimed he was very well-rounded with a wealth of knowledge. He had a good pregnancy rate, which elevated him in my rankings. A close family with a sister who was a dancer, a tall lawyer brother, a naval officer father and a green-eyed, strawberry blond mother. He was a physiologist with 3.6 grade point average and played the clarinet and cello.

The final candidate, Number 73, had even greater advantages. He was getting a PhD in pharmacology and was reputed to have a robust sense of humor. That I liked right away. He also sported a 4.0 grade point average and had secured numerous grants and scholarships. At six feet and 165 pounds, he was on the slender side, though Ginny vouched for his broad shoulders. His father was an engineer, his mother a librarian with a master's degree, and three sisters (a definite plus); an MBA, a writer, and a graphic artist. He did not drink or smoke, nor did he have allergies. And, yes, he sported a high sperm count and high rate of pregnancies in the program.

"He's my guy," I reported to Ava on the phone. "I like the idea of a smart kid who makes me laugh. I'm placing my order in the morning."

Thanksgiving

How was I going to tell my child his/her father's name is Number 73 and that I charged him on my Gold Mastercard? Well, I could truthfully say we met at the ballet. He was delivered on dry ice from California and I took a long lunch to bring him to meet our matchmaker, Dr. Varga, and leave him in his cold, customized nitrogen bath in the bowels of New York Hospital. The first insemination attempt was to take place the following week during my cycle's prime time. I would be alone. Ava was scheduled to leave Saturday for Argentina and Chile on business. My fertile times and her flight schedules were not in sync.

And how would I handle an infant and work when Madame Frequent Flyer was away? If we were sharing a home, stalwart Edith would be on duty. But if I remained living alone in my studio apartment? I banished the horror of that scenario from my mind. Instead, my daydream migrated to my own little house in Sag Harbor where I had not been in almost a month.

The simple cottage and luminous light of the area was unfailingly restorative. It sat on a quiet street that dead-ended at the estuary behind Long Beach, a mile outside the historic center of the town. I had bought the house the year I turned forty from an old woman who was moving into a retirement community after the deaths of her husband and son. A simple beach cottage that had been winterized in the early 70's, it had a woodburning stove that made the living room glow on winter nights and a deck that looked towards the bay. The sun set in varying hues of blue, pink, and orange over the saltwater creek that formed a pond at the end of the street.

Wouldn't Sag Harbor be a lovely place to raise a child, I mused? Maybe if I left the ballet and went back to consulting? But what about living with Ava and Elizabeth? As the reality of having a child grew it became more difficult to suppress my doubts about Ava's commitment. Perhaps I knew even then that I could not count on her.

Years later, I saw an IMAX film at the National Air and Space Museum in Washington, D.C. There, on a two-story high screen, I saw a creative yet scientific representation of the large and small wonders of the universe. During a few Technicolor moments, I plumbed the infinite number of worlds within worlds within a single drop of pond water, splitting the atom, nodding at quarks. And then, moments later, accompanied by deafening stereo surroundsound echoing the biggest bang, I was ejected up out of our solar system, beyond the Milky Way, onto the edge of known universes so that all we could ever hope to comprehend was still just a mote in the eye of God. And as I sat there, I nodded yes. This is how it felt to love Ava. From the core of unknowable beginnings, out beyond the edge of comprehension, as two bits of the stuff of the universe, swirling together, that is how our union felt. A loss of this magnitude was not easy to contemplate. But the thought of not being part of the great chain of being, of passing on the love I had experienced as a child to a child of my own had become equally unimaginable.

The second round of insemination attempts was scheduled for the day before and the day of the Joffrey gala at the Plaza Hotel. My first attempt had failed, and I was depressed for a week. If stress is a deterrent to insemination, as some holistic and psychologically-orientated practitioners would have it, I was doomed to an utterly fruitless attempt despite my having gone on Clomid, which promised to ripen and release enough eggs for an Easter egg hunt. Positioned in the stirrups in Dr. Varga's dimly lit office I watched him flip on the sonogram and commence his spelunking expedition. He pointed out the fat sacs with tendrils like creatures from the deep lagoon on the grainy black and white screen. "Look. Look at all those eggs!" he exclaimed joyfully. The sight of that forest of fat expectancy conjured scary images of quintuplets crawling up the walls of my studio apartment.

Once the now familiar plastic plug was inserted, I dressed and dashed across town to the ballet for a day crammed with ever-changing seating charts, hysterical artistic crises, commutes between the Plaza catering office and the theater, and the processing of checks in a frenzy to make that week's payroll. If any chubby embryo hung on through that, he/she was destined to become a one-person superpower. It was becoming clear to me that I needed to give up working in performing arts if I was going to become a mother; all those late nights and red-eye flights, the drama, the pressure. It wasn't only that I questioned that I'd have the energy for it all, I knew that I wanted to create a home as much like the one I grew up in as I could manage. I wanted to *be* with my child as much as possible. Part time work, fine, but full time, plus? No. Consulting it would be, then, despite the financial risk that implied.

Following the failure of the second round, Dr. Varga ordered a histogram, a procedure that would determine if my fallopian tubes were clear to allow for impregnation. There was some question about this as I had had surgery to remove fibroids several years earlier and the scar tissue might be responsible for inhibiting my ability to conceive. I wondered why he did not suggest this *before* I spent the first several thousand dollars and aged in all sorts of ways from the stress, but I went along with his recommendation and scheduled the procedure. I was committed to keep trying until at least the end of the year. Perhaps, by then a clear plan could be worked out with Ava.

Or not.

I asked for the first appointment of the day so I could make it to the ballet before most of the office staff showed up. Working for performing arts organizations was always a challenge to my biorhythms. By nature, I am an early riser and start dozing by ten at night. But the Artistic Director thought noon was a breakfast meeting and anyone leaving the office before 8:00 p.m. a slacker ...never mind that I arrived at 8:00 a.m. and did a half-day's work before he had opened an eye and reached for his toupée. I compensated by taking midafternoon naps in my tiny City Center office on performance nights and was grateful for the several hours of uninterrupted work I could get in early before the bill collectors started banging on the elevator door.

"Okay, Amanda/Alexander, this is Papa." I had acquired the habit of talking to the roving spirit of my yet-to-be conceived child. Just in case souls in between lives were shopping for a new body, I wanted to get their attention. At my age, and with frozen instead of "fresh" sperm, I needed all the spin I could get. From the literature I had gathered at the sperm bank on my California trip, I knew only 19 percent of insemination cases ended up as pregnancies.

Yes, in some ways it was better having anonymous Number 73 rather than an actual father. I could more convincingly imagine Ava as the other parent. In the dimmed light of his office, with me in the classic gynecological position in the stirrups, his Hungarian accented "Good luck," and quick kiss on the cheek as he depressed the plunger filled with Number 73 into my uterus, I could imagine the proper ethnic swirl at conception. Next time I would wear some of Ava's sandalwood perfume to enhance the aura. The plastic tampon plug Varga then inserted, which I had to suffer for the next three hours of meetings at the ballet, however, was decidedly unromantic.

***

Thanksgiving was Ava's favorite holiday. As soon as Elizabeth was home from school on Wednesday, they picked me up so that we could make our way to Connecticut before rush hour. The metallic beige Mercedes glided to a halt in front of my apartment building, parallel to the ever-present line of parked cars along the curb. Ava was skilled at the controls. She also had a pilot's license, although I had never flown with her. In my imagination we would glide like Robert Redford and Meryl Streep, holding hands in an open biplane over the Serengeti above rippling herds of wildebeests and flamingos in vistas laced with predatory lunges and ruthless beauty.

The lid of the trunk eased open.

"Careful, darling, there are a lot of groceries for Thanksgiving," said Ava as I squeezed between car bumpers with my bag. Elizabeth was jumping up and down in the back seat with Kaiser Wilhelm, and Edith, the housekeeper, was sitting impassively to the side, eyes heavy lidded, hands folded, nursing her hangover.

I eased into the tawny leather front seat and leaned over for a greeting kiss. Ava exuded the freshness of the newly showered with an overlay of sandalwood. Though dressed casually in her light jeans and cotton turtleneck, she did not look American. Maybe it was her elegantly tailored jacket and the tan Italian leather pumps.

"Mind if we stop for coffee?" I asked.

Ava smiled her pursed lip smile that verged on a kiss. "You must stop that, darling, if you are serious about your 'project.' you know." Project was her code for baby in public, which struck me as cold blooded rather than cute.

"But I'm still on hiatus. I'll quit again, don't worry." And how are you going to hide and/or explain the "project" once she/he arrives? I wondered.

"Ach. These delays are not good. You're not getting any younger."

"But better all the time," I teased back with an arched eyebrow. I was determined to stifle my misgivings and have a lighthearted holiday

Ava was worried about my health. Just as well that she had been out of town for the histogram. It had been the single most painful experience of my life, and I have a high threshold for pain. The repeated attempts to shoot liquid into the blocked fallopian tube caused such torturous agony that I cried out loud like a woman in late stages of childbirth. I could barely walk afterwards and was weak with the aftereffects for days.

Then, there was the laparoscopic surgery in September. My left fallopian tube was blocked by scar tissue from an old fibroid operation; hence the pain I experienced during the histogram. The scar tissue needed to be removed, along with a new fibroid brought on by the fertility drugs I had been taking. Ava had come to the hospital with me. I knew what a large gesture it was for her. She hated hospitals and sickness but wanted to show her support. She had costumed herself in a new designer outfit complete with appropriate jewelry. She looked fabulous. I found myself wondering in the cab on the way down Park Avenue when I would inherit that green suit. When Ava stayed home from her office on Yom Kippur and cleaned her closets, my own wardrobe improved dramatically. For someone in the not-for-profit world, I cut quite a figure in her one-year-old outfits—some of which she had never even worn—gathered on Madison Avenue, Paris, Berlin, and Buenos Aries. Ava believed that being well dressed signaled power and authority; authority she just might have to exercise in the hospital on my behalf.

The surgery itself went well enough, but I had a violent reaction to the anesthesia. When I finally came to in the recovery room, I was alone. All the other outpatients had been cleared for release while I languished in my drugged-out state. I awoke vomiting. It went on so long they thought they might have to keep me overnight for dehydration. Ava stepped in and insisted she take me home.

Tucked into the sofa bed in Ava's study, I continued my wretched cycle of dry heaves and replenishing liquids supplied by a concerned and clucking Edith at regular intervals. I had to wait until December or January for my uterus to heal before trying the next insemination. So much for having babies the "natural" way. Just as well, I told myself, to lay low during the holidays, which were stressful enough in their own right.

The hiatus halted my onward rush to conceive and forced me to acknowledge other sobering roadblocks to motherhood. I was already past forty, and an uncertain and expensive road to conceiving a baby lay before me. Should I let myself consider adoption after all? How ironic. After all the conflicts and struggles that I had worked through because of my lack of blood connection, would I now turn around and inflict that pain on another? But maybe that was the better route to motherhood for everyone involved after all. I knew the dark side of adoption, and perhaps by blending my heritage in a loving family along with a non-threatened stance about my child's own biological difference from me, I could help another child navigate that split with minimal pain. Ava had suggested adoption after the first round of failed insemination attempts, which I had rebuffed at the time. I was now ready to continue that conversation, perhaps this very weekend once the guests had cleared out.

***

"I'm making a cake," announced Elizabeth.

Edith set out the bowl, measuring spoons, egg, and milk; sort of like a valet setting out the master's clothes for the day. I never got the hang of what to do around live-in help. At Ava's I settled for making my bed, but not scouring the sink; clearing my plate from the table, but not loading the dishwasher. I thought about offering to make the sweet potatoes, but Edith was already at work on them. Tackling the bird itself was too major. Ava swooped through the kitchen melting butter, stirring a sauce, and poking the browning bird with the shiny prongs of the German cutlery. I opted for being Elizabeth's sous chef.

"Making something from your cookbook?" I asked.

"Yes. The fudge cake," she nodded. Elizabeth had bestowed upon me a copy of the recipe book she created at school, bound with yarn, and sporting a purple hand colored cover. "Can you hold the bowl?"

"Sure."

Elizabeth commenced blending the egg into the flour mix, her tongue poked out on the left side of her mouth to steady her effort. A surge of love for her washed over me.

A few weeks before, Ava had given me the greatest gift of our years together. We were eating dinner at a place on the West Side on one of our nights out when Elizabeth was with her father, when Ava looked up from her linguini and announced that she had been to her lawyer that afternoon.

"Something wrong?" I had asked. "Something with the business?" I knew she had been having problems with a supplier in Sicily who defaulted on a delivery of lemon concentrate to a supplier.

"No, darling, not that," she replied. "I changed my will."

"You're not ill, are you?" A shot of pure fear coursed through my system.

"No, no, nothing like that. It was time to update it. I needed to change some things. If something ever does happen to me, you will be Elizabeth's guardian along with Tom."

She might be having trouble integrating our life together, but she loved me and trusted me as much as she was capable of. She said all that and more by her action. And yet, all that bonding with Elizabeth would only be allowed once she was dead. Ava died fifteen years ago. Elizabeth was twenty-two then and not legally required to have a guardian at all. Without anyone's sanction or approval, Elizabeth and I have enjoyed an unbroken relationship, for which I will always be grateful.

"I'll check the lower oven to see if it's at the right temperature for the cake," I said to Elizabeth as she poured the batter.

I brushed Ava's shoulder as I bent over at the oven and smiled up at her. Her face was an impassive mask. She was elsewhere, concentrating on tasks to be done. It was difficult if not impossible for her to exude any warmth towards me with other people present. I wished she could overcome that mode, but I was accustomed to her Germanic formality from my own childhood. My mother's contained efficiency was a demonstration of caring that manifested more like a CEO and less like Mother Earth. What was it with these women born along the Danube? Papa was the one in our household who radiated affection and embraced the world at large. Mama's love was both less expansive and more selective. That she loved me more than any being on earth, I had no doubt. The same with Ava. I believed her when she told me that she had never wanted to make a life with anyone before me; that she only really cared about Elizabeth and me of all the population of the earth. I had possessed the love of a woman who did not love easily or openly once before. I was used to this. But Ava was not Marie Walton Veto. She had no track record of long-term relationships. In my world, a household that included two children was as serious a long term a commitment as I could imagine. I was ready for all the compromise and sacrifices that would come with blended family formation. Was Ava?

"Oven's ready," I reported to Elizabeth as she glided carefully towards me, balancing the cake pan.

"Want to play 'Clue'?" she asked once she slid the pan into the oven.

"Sure," I agreed. Elizabeth was a mystery devotee. She had the full set of Nancy Drew books in her room. When she got a little older, I planned to take her to one of those mystery weekends at a lodge in Westchester.

"Don't forget the cake," said Ava. "And setting the table. Everyone will be here at two."

We promised as we dashed up the stairs with Kaiser Wilhelm at our heels.

***

The cancellations started around eleven. Kaylie Jones, the one close friend of mine who was going to be part of the holiday, was coming down with bronchitis and had to stay in bed in New York. Ava's friend, the other Hungarian Ava, met a Korda cousin and his friend at Avis to drive up together only to be told their car had mistakenly been given to someone else and no others were available on Thanksgiving.

The group shrank to Ava's business partner and his family, a sculptor and his psychologist wife, and a wealthy retired businessman and his young wife. The women were part of a group Ava took long walks with on Saturday mornings. I had been to both of their homes to dinner parties as a houseguest of Ava's, so I had a nodding acquaintance with them. I had also seen Enrico many times at the office, but it was the first time I met his young Argentine wife and six-year-old son. I decided that it was my duty as secret co-hostess to chat her up and make introductions while Ava was engaged with Enrico and Robert, a sculptor, on the other side of the room near the fireplace.

"You must meet Renee, Maria. She does a lot of work with children and adolescents in her practice," I suggested as I guided her to where Renee was stationed with John, the retired business magnate who had a passion for literature.

"How do you know each other?" Maria asked brightly of the group in general. She lived in New Jersey and was more likely to commute to Buenos Aires or Europe than to keep a second home in Connecticut or the Hamptons like the bulk of New Yorkers of a certain set.

"Homes near here. The dinner party circuit makes it a small town," explained John.

"Yes, I've noticed that," I offered. "Same sort of thing in the Hamptons."

"Oh, so you don't have a house here?"

"No, I have a house in Sag Harbor. I live in New York. Near Ava."

At that moment Elizabeth joined the conversation group in the living room, buying me extra time to regroup for an answer, and snaked an arm around my waist. At eleven, she already came up past my shoulder. She would be very tall, like her father.

"How's school, Elizabeth?" John asked heartily.

"Fine," shrugged Elizabeth. I suppressed a smile. Elizabeth and I joked about how grown-ups usually had only two questions: "How old are you?" and "How's school?"

"How do you know Ava?" Maria persisted as she sipped her wine.

"We're good friends," I replied.

"Where did you meet?"

"Meet?" I was not used to this question in casual conversation. The group turned to me politely for my answer. We had met at a fund-raising casino night for gay charities. Ava had targeted me from the moment of her entrance and we were in bed and in love within two weeks.

"It was at a charity event in the Hamptons several years ago," I said finally, after rapidly editing the story in my head.

"I never knew that," piped in Elizabeth.

"You were away at camp," I said lightly. "I met you a month or so later. Here. You never got out of the pool the whole weekend, remember?"

"Yeah, I think so. But I thought Mom said you met in New York at Janos's house."

"Will you excuse us?" I said hastily. Renee had a quizzical look on her face, and I did not want to find out Ava had told her yet another version of this story during one of their walks. "I want to help Edith reset the table. And Elizabeth needs to check on her dessert surprise."

I quickly led Elizabeth away through the dining room and into the kitchen. How was I going to raise a child in a house where my status was houseguest? How could I tell the truth to my child when Elizabeth was told a different story? What use was a beautiful house that was featured in *Town & Country* when you had to sleep in the guest wing?

"It looks great, Elizabeth," I said, spinning the cake around on its plate. "It's cool enough to ice now, I think."

"I can do it, Janine, if you want to go out and be with the grown-ups."

"No, I'd rather be here with you," I said brightly.

"I know," said Elizabeth. She reached to cover the hand I had clenched on the countertop and gave it a squeeze. "We can play Clue again when they leave, okay? Maybe you can win this time."

"Hey, how do you know I didn't *let* you win, huh?" I said.

"Ha!" exclaimed Elizabeth. "Fat chance. I know you."

Elizabeth, in the playroom, with a wrench to the heart. Edith, in the kitchen, with a bottle of gin. Ava, in the bedroom, with a single bullet in a revolver, twirling. All the safety experts agree: the most dangerous place to be is in one's own home.

Sanctuary

Chicago's O'Hare Airport. It is called a hub now. As a child, I had thrilled to the attribution, "Busiest Airport in the World." Each year, in the dankest part of February, my mother, brother, and I would escort my father to the airport for his four-week buying trip in Europe. Each February, my imagination left with him and danced through Paris, Rome, London, Athens, Florence, Barcelona, Vienna, and Zurich. Each day after school, I'd run home to rip open the blue onion skin envelopes and read my father's reports in his block capital printing about an evening at the Dior table at the Folies Bregère; a tour of the Parthenon; a formal dinner starting at 10:00 p.m. on the lace-making island of Madeira. Each letter would conclude with his longing for home and family. Wait, wait, my ten-year-old self would scream inside—the wrong person is traveling! Papa wants to be home and it is I, *I* who should be threading my way through Europe.

And then, in March, a second Christmas would be celebrated in our home. Papa would return with a gift from every city he had visited; physical proof that his heart remained with his family every single day of his travels. Mantillas from Spain for church (black for my mother, pink for me); a tiny replica of the Vienna Opera House for my silver charm bracelet which already dangled a Dutch windmill, a blue enameled crest from Sweden and a replica of Big Ben. An inlaid side table from Capri; a mandolin-shaped music box that played "O Sol o Mio;" Irish linen table cloths; twisted Venetian glass wine goblets; fine leather gloves and silk ties; postcards of mountain scenes and statuary; a souvenir program from LaScala; a box of fine linen handkerchiefs embroidered with a "J."

Our reunion would happen here, at O'Hare, with Bob and me fidgeting and the ever-calm Marie standing outside the customs door. The travelers were different then, too; more decorous. No blue jeans and sneakers; no backpacks and wheeled carry-ons. No trails of wailing children, strollers, and stray diaper bags. It was a dignity of dark wool and subtle tweeds. Men in fedoras with leather briefcases and women in mink and fine hose.

The airport was smaller as well as less hectic then, too. No entire terminal devoted to United Airlines like I found myself in now—vaulted ceilings of exposed girders and glass. A descent, and then a long, moving conveyer belt transporting me through a light show of neon and electronic music reminiscent of the disco on the beach of Punta del Este where I had been last Christmas with Ava. Her and Ava's routine would keep Elizabeth there for a full three weeks. And this year, I had not been invited to join them.

No, this Christmas I was the child coming home. Alone. Not one half of a new family. I was healed from the operation and could try insemination again in January, but I hesitated to make the next appointment. It was not just the expense and uncertain outcomes of trying for a pregnancy. My view of how I wanted to parent was evolving. Just because I had let myself feel the powerful urge most humans possess to have a physical child that carried my own genes did not mean that I had to follow that path. As I drew closer to motherhood, I realized that what I had to give as a parent was more important than what I could "get" for my own ego or curiosity. I had biological relatives now, thanks to my search, and did not feel so compelled to give birth myself. And who was better equipped than me to raise an adopted child? I would not be threatened by curiosity about birth parents; I would understand the mysterious pain the child would bear. I would not expect the child to be like me in talents or interests or even ethnicity.

At the ground-floor baggage claim I retrieved my suitcase from the carousel and peered down the long terminal corridor. Where was my mother? A woman of efficiency and time-proven routines, Marie Walton Veto was supposed to be at the baggage claim and my father in the car outside, ready to make another circle around the airport if the police thought he was occupying the curbside pick-up for too long. So, it had been for over twenty years. Part of coming home was a return to the reliability of just this sort of ritual.

"Janine Veto, please meet your party at the United Airlines courtesy desk," suggested the calm, midwestern voice over the paging system. I set my suitcase on edge and wheeled it down to the counter. Yes, there was my mother, her small frame swathed in the red plaid coat she had bought sometime early in the previous decade. In her gloved hand she held a scrap of paper, probably one from her homemade pads of old calendar pages with a 'good side' still begging to be used. I smiled, but in the moment before my mother's face lit up with recognition, I saw the lost, bewildered gaze of an old woman, a look that pierced my heart even when I saw it on strangers; that hesitation and confusion of a frail figure swaying at the fare box of a city bus, clawing at a worn change purse with arthritic fingers as a bustling, oh-so-important line of commuters pushed and agitated behind her. That gaze of frail ladies sitting at Formica lunch counters at indifferent coffee shops, waiting for their check or a refill; waiting, and forgetting just why.

"Janine, you're here!" exclaimed my mother.

I bent down to enfold her in a hug. The United agent nodded and caught my eye.

"We found your mother upstairs at departures and thought she might have better luck down here."

"Departures?"

The agent nodded. "Yes. But she had this paper with the flight number on it, so we escorted her here to the desk."

"Thank you so much," I said. "Lucky thing she didn't write it in shorthand."

"Oh, but I don't write numbers in shorthand, darling, only words." The twinkle had returned to my mother's blue eyes.

"Ah, it's mystery writing to me, Mama. Always was." I met the young man's eyes above my mother's head and exchanged a knowing look with him. My mother had been lost. The connective pattern of intent had not held during the space of time that it took her to walk from the car to the baggage carousel. Thank God for Marie Veto's training as an executive secretary that still had her taking notes on anything that came to her over the phone. My mother disguised her galloping dementia by leaving cryptic shorthand notes around the house reminding her of calls to be made, appointments to the hairdresser or doctor, laundry to do, and bills to be paid.

I took my mother's hand to lead her to the door and felt a scrape against my wrist. Startled, I looked down. Long fingernails, yellowed as old lace, curled inward towards her palm. My mother's nails had always been so crisply trimmed and filed. Nails had been an issue of debate between us when my teenaged self was experimenting with the painting and hair teasing trappings of femininity. "Janine, why don't you cut those nails," my mother would shudder. "You look like Fu Manchu."

"Put on your gloves, Mama," I said as we approached the airport exit. The knife-edge cold smote me on the forehead with a numbing blow. My mother did not seem to notice. Was my own blood thinner, or was my eighty-eight-year-old mother hardier than me? I had an only partially jesting theory that my parents were living to such advanced ages precisely because they did not retire to Florida's warmth. They were both half frozen. If you transplanted them to a semi-tropical climate they would defrost and die within a matter of weeks.

I spotted my father's gray fedora where he stood guard next to their late model Oldsmobile. After we hugged and stowed my suitcase in the trunk, I ducked into the back seat. Papa guided the car smoothly out of the airport and onto the expressway. I sat in the back and surveyed the familiar flat landscape on either side under a cast iron sky.

"I need to pick up a few things at Dominick's on the way home, honey. Anything you want?" asked my mother, as the car left the expressway.

"Just coffee, Mama. I'm sure you have everything else."

Papa raised his eyebrow at me in the rearview mirror at her comment, but I kept silent. In the grocery store parking lot, he eased the car up to the front near the entrance and pulled into a handicap parking spot. He enjoyed this perk of old age and rickety limbs. Mama hopped out of the car and did her prancing step over the icy spots on her way to the door. No one could convince her prancing was more dangerous than sure-footed steps on slick surfaces. She would nod sweetly at the advice and go right on ice dancing.

I slid into the front seat next to my father and casually shuffled through the glove compartment. "Oh, my God. Is this what I think it is?" I pulled out a long piece of light cardboard. It was a hand rendered map of Mt. Carmel and Queen of Heaven Cemeteries, with all the familial graves clearly indicated. Here were Papa's parents and the infant brother and sister who had died in the flu pandemic of 1918. Further off, toward the newer section, were all four of Papa's older brothers. A nephew, on Mama's side, who died of a brain aneurysm and failed kidneys. The two husbands of Mama's living sisters and her sister Jeannette, the youngest of her family and the only Republican, who died of cancer almost ten years before. And, further to the side beneath the outstretched arms of the Blessed Virgin, were the plots for Marie and Emil Veto, bought and paid for twenty years ago. In the past year, however, the deed for those plots—along with a thorough list of whom was to get what family heirloom and brief obit copy—had all been moved to a portfolio on top of Mama's desk.

"How's she doing, Papa?"

"Oh, there are good days and bad days."

I folded the map and snapped the glove compartment shut.

"What's taking her so long?" I mused, as I gazed at the panoramic windows of the grocery store through the ice-ringed windshield.

"Oh, it always does, honey. Don't worry. She has her list."

"Her list?"

"Sure. She writes down what we need, and she goes down the list and gets the item no matter where it is in the store, and then goes on to the next thing."

I exchanged a look with my father. "Is this how she gets her exercise?"

"Something like that. I get a nap and she gets out a little. It's okay. I've talked to the store manager. They know about her."

With my mother, Marie Walton Veto.

I nodded and took a breath. "Papa, I don't think United Airlines knows about her, though. Today, well, the 'list' with the flight number saved her, but she was lost. Really lost. I don't know if we can let her do that again."

Papa shook his head. His hearing aid caught my eye nestled into the hollow of his big ear. As a little girl I would crawl into his lap and whisper into that welcoming chamber and tickle the dark ear hairs to produce a belly laugh that would create a child-sized earthquake on his lap. "I don't know, honey. If you mention these things to her, or how often she repeats things, right after she says them, well, sometimes she cries."

"Let me see how she's doing, okay?" I had a sudden urge to hover protectively over my mother. I shivered as I emerged from the car. The glass front of the grocery store stretched half the width of the parking lot. This was another re-entry exercise for me, this midwestern profligacy with space. All these elongated buildings with wide aisles that any self-respecting New Yorker would stand on edge and compress.

I found my mother in the soup aisle examining the label on a can of Progresso Penne with Chicken.

"You have to read the labels, you know," my mother explained. "Your father can't have too much sodium and so many of these soups are loaded with it."

"Let me see," I said. Sure enough; over 900 mg. of sodium. "Too bad. This looks like one he'd like. So, what is it? Back to bland Campbell's low sodium tomato and chicken noodle? Maybe you can put some herbs in it or beans and turkey sausage or something."

Mama reached for the Campbell's soup and started slowly reading the label. If my mother could still get it together to cook beans and turkey sausage separately and then put them into soup, she could cook a whole meal rather than rely on nutrition in a can.

"Okay, Mom, can I help? Let me see your list. How about if I get the ice cream?"

"No, honey, I always get the ice cream and milk last, so it won't spoil."

"Spoil? Mom, it's eight degrees outside—way below zero with wind chill—and we're six blocks from home."

Mama gave me a beatific smile. "You're just like your father. He's always trying to put things into the basket."

"Okay, I get the message," I laughed. "Mind if I just tag along, then?"

I took over steering the shopping cart and followed my mother through the labyrinthine course of her journey.

That night I unpacked my suitcase into a drawer that my father had cleared for me in the dresser of my old bedroom. The room had undergone several transformations over the years; the pink walls papered over with a pale green patterned wallpaper more suitable for adults. It had too much furniture in it now. In fact, the entire house felt overloaded from the recent combining of my parents' two households. That summer they had sold the Wisconsin lake house where they had spent half their time for the twenty-five years since my father's retirement.

I sat on the edge of the bed that was draped with a faded rose and green bedspread I remembered from Wisconsin. It must have been the very one that was used in the back bedroom that overlooked the forest in the rear of the house; the room in which I woke up nearly two decades earlier during another journey when I had flown to seek my mother's help in searching for Bev.

I maintain that the Wisconsin lake house added ten years to my father's life. With their increasing infirmity, however, my parents had sold the house earlier that very year and moved back permanently to the Villa Park house. Ever practical, they had installed the central air conditioning they would need now that piney lake breezes would no longer cool the summer air. The house was painted and thermal pane windows installed to keep the winter's arctic blasts at bay. Old chairs were reupholstered. Their world, with all their earthly possessions, had shrunk to the lot line of their quarter acre plot at the corner of Villa Avenue and Oak Street. Twilight was deepening to dusk.

"More coffee?" I stood next to my mother's chair at the kitchen table the first morning of my visit. I had the Farberware coffee maker that used to reside in the lake house poised over her cup. "Perk" coffee reigned in the Veto home. Whole beans, grinding, drip, and the entire urban status sorter based on how you got your Joe was alien in this kitchen.

"Oh, just a little." Mama held the rooster-patterned cup with both hands. It was part of a set that I later inherited. I have had many compliments on my taste in retro chic thanks to those dishes and the bamboo-framed furniture with original floral upholstery with which I decorated my Sag Harbor house a decade later.

"Good. And I'll get you another ice cube."

"So, there won't be any left for lunch?"

"Oh, Mama, I'll have made a whole other pot by then. Don't worry." I smiled.

"How about me?" chirped Papa from his place across the table.

"Now, Papa, don't be naughty. I'll put on more water for your *decaf* tea. Sit. I want to talk with you a minute."

I took a deep breath. "I'm seriously thinking. No, *planning* to have a child."

"What?" my mother's mouth went from the exclamation into a half moon smile in rapid succession. I chanced looking her right in the eye, only to discover that she was not as surprised as I had anticipated. I tended to underestimate how well my mother knew me.

"How will you manage?" asked my father, his default jovial expression folding into wrinkled concern. "Your work, your health?

"I'm working it all out, Papa. I have Ava's support and I can always go back to consulting and work part-time. I can rent out the Sag Harbor house for income. I'll manage."

"But you need insurance," he continued. "Both of you. You can't be without it."

"Emil. It will be fine," my mother said firmly as her gaze drifted to a place somewhere over my head. "Raising the children was the happiest part of my married life."

"Oh, thanks a lot," said Papa, shifting to his comic mode and acquiescence to my mother's position of authority regarding family matters.

"No, no, it overcame me when I was almost forty. It was what I wanted more than anything in the world. Why wouldn't Janine feel it, too? Go ahead, honey. I'm just sorry that we'll be so far away, but we will help if we can."

I looked at my mother and followed her gaze. Her eyes were resting on the wooden plaque over the door to the dining room I had gotten for them twenty-five years before when I was living in Honolulu after college. It was the Chinese character "shou," for Longevity. So, it had worked, thus far, I mused. In Chinese lore, the God of Long Life was one of the prime gods of Happiness. He holds the peach of immortality in his hand, decides the hour of death for each person and writes it on his tablet. But it can be changed. What did I have to do to keep these loving people here long enough to see the grandchild they had long ago given up hope of seeing from me?

It was already too late to hope for their active participation. What they had given my brother's children would not be possible for mine. They had taken each of Bob's three children, one at a time in rotation over the summers of their growing up. My father renamed the stretch of sand by the water every several weeks: Suzie Beach, Tina Beach, Craig Beach. He piloted them on endless fishing trips on the pontoon boat and constructed "chipmunk circuses" for them as he had done for Bob and me when were children.

For my child there would be no memories of summer days on the lake followed by cool nights in Grandma's house with special drawers for each child that were kept, untouched, for their private stash of childhood treasurers between visits. The house was gone, and soon my parents would be as well. Was there enough time to add one more name to the family bassinet nestled in the storeroom, carefully covered with plastic while my mother still had the mental faculty to read it and my father the strength to lift the baby from its shallow, padded comfort?

It was during those December days in my childhood home that my focus firmly shifted from childbearing to adoption. I had come to see it as a profound response to the call to pass on all the positives of my own experience enhanced by my familiarity with the dark side of adoption. Underlying my resolve was my parents' love that felt like a program always running in the background of my life.

On New Year's Eve, 1992, back home in New York I put away my volume of *What to Expect When You're Expecting,* stored my files on Dr. Varga and fertility clinics, and opened the yellow pages to adoption agencies.

The Real Estate Section

520 East 84th Street, Apartment 2J

Studio apartment, second floor in elevator building (no doorman), facing street on shady residential street. Wood floors. Approx. 650 sq. ft. Rent stabilized.

The renewal lease arrived shortly after the first of the year, the day after I had called Spence-Chapin adoption services and requested a package of material on its program. I had ninety days in which to respond. I put the lease into my "to do" folder. Ava and I had not spoken about moving in together for several months, and it was not a good time to bring it up. She was feeling pressured; did not want any more decisions or changes until after she sold her business; after she decided about Elizabeth going to boarding school; after the next trip to Argentina. Maybe we could talk about it in February when Ava, Elizabeth, and I were going to Utah on a ski vacation—my first. Having grown up in the midwest, I had never learned to ski. I imagined us clad in turtlenecks underneath loose knit sweaters, rosy cheeked and relaxed by a roaring fire. Then we could talk about it. A lifetime of family gatherings in front of the fire . . . in New York, Connecticut, Sag Harbor? All had fireplaces. Only my studio was lacking one.

A week later I fell victim to that year's strain of flu and took to my bed. Ava arrived after work and briskly unpacked a grocery bag brimming with cans of soup, ginger ale, Pepperidge Farm Milano cookies, bread, tea, and fruit.

"The fluids are most important, darling," she instructed me. I smiled feverishly. It was comforting to have her there.

"Mind getting the mail?" I asked. "The box is so small, if you let even one day go by, everything gets jammed up and twisted in there."

"Of course,"

Flipping through *The New Yorker,* Con Edison bill, and fund-raising appeals, I came to a large white envelope with Spence-Chapin stamped in blue on the return address.

"The adoption material," I announced to Ava, who was warming up soup in the tiny kitchen. I ripped open the envelope and quickly scanned the pages. They offered both domestic and international adoption. The latter listed the countries with which they had relationships and the criteria that each country imposed on prospective parents. Many restricted adoptions to married couples. Some had an age limit of forty. Others included a religious stipulation.

"Let's see," said Ava as she placed a small table next to the bed for the soup. She fluffed up my pillows behind me as I wiggled up to a sitting position, then sat next to me to examine the papers.

"So. With domestic they act as a counselor. They really don't have the babies, right?"

"I don't want to go that route, anyway," I said. "I'm uncomfortable with the notion of having to compete for the favors of a frightened teenage girl. Things have changed since I was adopted. There are relatively few white babies available and it is as competitive as trying to get into an uppity New York City pre-school. Why would a girl choose me, a single woman past forty over all the young couples who want her baby? No, that doesn't feel right to me. I'm more attracted to the international anyway."

"Which country?" Ava flipped the pages back and forth as she analyzed the choices.

"From what I understand from my conversation on the phone—and these papers seem to confirm it—I'm eligible for Paraguay, Ecuador, China, and Russia."

"Russia?" Ava looked up with interest.

"Yes, but only for children with 'special needs.' I don't know if I'm equipped for that. Sure, sure, once you have a child, you accept whatever happens. But to start out that way? And besides, I'm a little afraid of the fetal alcohol problem there."

"So." Ava nodded. "With Paraguay or Ecuador, it would be good with the Spanish, with both Elizabeth and me speaking it. And we'd be in Argentina at least part of the time."

"No, actually, what draws me is China," I said. "It just feels right. And they're all girls. The one child policy, you know. Hundreds of thousands of girls abandoned in the hopes that the next child will be a boy."

Besides the social justice issue of pushing back against a culture that favored boys over girls, I had my own personal reasons for embracing the adoption of a child of another race. I remembered my emotional confusion and anxiety from my own childhood when people would comment on how I looked like my mother (which was not objectively true) or resembled another member of my extended family. Each time I had to choose whether to correct their genetic assumption and make a point of my outsider status, or remain silent, which felt like deception. I liked the idea of having the issue obvious to all so that my daughter would not have to navigate between that Scylla and Charybdis. How was I to know that during her adolescence her ethnic difference from me thrust her into a no man's land as an outsider of *both* American and Chinese culture? Her obvious difference from me did not give her the choice of revealing her adoption status or not. I knew that adoption blew a hole through the soul that requires healing, but I was ignorant of what additional damage would be inflicted with the double-barreled blast of interracial adoption.

"Well, the Chinese are intelligent, and she'd probably be healthy with that diet. Besides, she wouldn't be affected by the alcohol problem or the narcotic leaves the Indians chew in Central America."

"Or venereal disease or AIDS," I responded. I looked at Ava. She was using "we" a lot in the conversation.

"So, what next?" she asked.

"A general orientation meeting. They have them several times a year. You must make a reservation. The next one is in May, I think."

"It is good that you get all the information. Half of having children is figuring out the logistics."

I nodded. The next day I made a reservation for two at the session in May.

In April, the *New York Times Magazine*'s cover story featured the plight of Chinese baby girls and documented the adoption journey of an American couple to southern China. I caught my breath when I opened the paper that Sunday. The baby was so beautiful, fresh, and ancient at the same time.

My heart leapt. Yes. This was the way I wanted to go. Then, another fear rose up. Now that this story was plastered all over the paper, there would be a stampede at the adoption agencies! Everyone would want to adopt Chinese baby girls. The old notion of scarcity and competition took hold. Damn. Why couldn't the article have come out in June, after my Spence-Chapin meeting. After I got in there for first dibs?

By the time the May meeting approached, logic had stepped in. Even if the article caused a surge in interest in China, only sixty people could attend the next intake meeting at Spence-Chapin, which was over half full when I had made my own reservation. As it turned out, only fifty-nine people were in attendance that evening. Ava had declined to attend. She was in one of her pulling back phases; so much so that I had silently signed my renewal lease and put in into the mail at the beginning of May.

It was an eclectic group of people that gathered that evening in the Upper East Side. Ages varied from the thirties to the sixties, mostly couples, but several single women and a few single men. Sitting in rows of folding chairs, we listened as the heads of the domestic, African American, and international divisions gave brief presentations and passed out literature.

I shivered as I heard of the process for the domestic route that involved placing plaintive ads in newspapers in strategic locales throughout the country pitched at pregnant girls in whose hands the entire decision would rest. This new era of "open" U.S. adoption was no more appealing to me than my own beginnings in the secret dungeons of ecclesiastical shame.

My attention perked up considerably when Flicka van Praugh took over to explain the international program. Slender, bespectacled, gray hair held back on one side with a bobby pin, Flicka was the WASP head mistress from Central Casting. She reviewed all the criteria I was already familiar with from the literature and fielded questions from those who had not read the material as closely as I had, about ages of eligibility for specific countries, marital status and, in some cases, religion.

Then, without prompting of any sort, she fixed her gaze at a space just above the heads in the middle of our group and stated, "Of course, no country wants to *knowingly* give a child to a gay parent. However, I am not going to ask that question. You are not going to volunteer that information. And I never said any of this." She allowed her eyes to drift down to our faces then, a slight smile at the corners of her mouth as she seamlessly led into an explanation of how to fill out the simple form if we were still interested and arrange for an intake interview.

Now, this was a woman I could work with. I filled out my form, chatted briefly with a few other prospective parents and walked back the dozen blocks to my apartment, humming.

Roxbury CT.

Historic house restored and enhanced on five acres. Separate pool house and office cabin. Six bedrooms, four baths, den, family room, eat-in kitchen, two fireplaces. Featured in Town & Country.

Ava and I had not been alone in six weeks, with holidays and business trips juggling the schedule. Even the ski trip we had planned was cancelled when Elizabeth tripped over Kaiser Wilhelm in the hall of the apartment and broke her foot. So, despite a snowfall that threatened to turn to ice, Ava and I headed up to Connecticut on a Friday night for a much-needed time of quiet and companionship.

The temperature continued to drop as we made our way up the Sawmill Parkway. It was always less crowded on the highways up to Connecticut than out to the Hamptons via the Long Island Expressway on weekends. And, on a night this forbidding, the highway was as deserted as a country road. When we left the well-tended interstate in Southbury, the hard snow-packed streets were dotted with patches of ice that shimmered in the reflection of light from streetlamps lining the exit. Ava flexed her gloved hands on the wheel and focused on the dark road ahead that led past the shopping center, through the edge of town and then up to the crest of a steep hill where we'd turn off towards the house. At the base of the last, long hill Ava shifted into low gear. We made it halfway up the incline before the car hesitated and started spinning its wheels as is slid slowly back down.

"Whoa," I exclaimed. "And this is a Mercedes."

"Don't worry, darling. We're not done yet." Ava's concentration doubled as she gunned the powerful engine and took on the hill once again. And again. On the third attempt we were just about to cross the critical last few yards before the crest of the hill when the treacherous ice sabotaged our ascent once again. We slid sideways down to the right and off the road. The car's rear end firmly planted itself into a bank of three-foot high snow.

"That's it!" Ava pronounced.

"Time for AAA," I countered. I fished my card out of my wallet and Ava called from the car phone. They could not get to us for more an hour, so we decided to walk the last half mile to the house and have them pick us up there.

The air was sharp, but not frigid. I gulped the cold deep into my lungs and fell into rhythmic step behind Ava up the slope that had defeated the epitome of German engineering. At the crest of the hill, we paused, triumphant. Ava and I embraced in victory then turned down the road we had traversed so many times on our morning walks from her house. Overhead, ice encrusted limbs clacked against each other in the wind, twigs illuminated intermittently by a sliver of moon dodging silently in and out of swollen indigo clouds overhead. It was a stroll in magic time. Ava was a creature of mountain ice and desert sand. Away from the sophisticated world she navigated so well, her spirit shone. A silent current ran between us. I turned. Her silvery laughter crackled through the air. I wanted nothing more than to have this perfect moment suspended for all my days on earth.

If she had asked me then, would I have given up pursuing the baby?

Park Avenue, the Eighties
Classic six with three bedrooms; two baths with maid's room and bath off eat-in kitchen.

I lay awake on the sofa bed in Ava's study and tried to imagine it as my new home in the city. Although it was nearly the end of March, a sudden and prolific snowstorm enveloped the city. Instead of charging up to Connecticut, we had decided to stay in New York. Elizabeth and I ventured out during the height of the storm to Radio Shack to get speaker wire to fix the CD player. Ava was always impressed when I did these little repairs. And I, in turn, felt more a part of the "family" scene. It felt normal to putter. What was hard for me to get used to was having hired help do every little thing. Like the time the previous summer I suggested to Elizabeth that we wash the cars. She had looked at me quizzically. The concept was not within her realm of experience. Mercedes' were washed by garage attendants off Park Avenue for twenty-five dollars a pop. So much for trying to share the happy memories of my brother Bob and me washing down the 1955 Pontiac Star Chief with my father and drying it with the tawny chamois cloth that soaked up the water with magical ease. Oh, and the times we would wax the car and watch the creamy swirls of wax give way to shiny brilliance, then stand back, drinking lemonade to admire our work. Or the talks my father and I would have down in his workroom in the basement when we polished the family shoes on the weekend. It was that same satisfaction of bringing out a shine through the layer of pasty dullness.

There was enough room for me in the study, I pondered, but where would I put a crib? In truth, this room would be perfect as a nursery for the baby if I could sleep with Ava in the queen-sized bed in the large bedroom with two walk-in closets. Her bedroom was connected to the study through one bathroom and connected to Elizabeth's room through another full bath. Yes, that would be fine if we could live as a couple in the center, with our daughters' rooms radiating to either side. But that configuration was consistently rejected by Ava.

I sighed and turned over. Somehow, being the "secret" choice did not help. The previous week Ava, Elizabeth and I had had a lovely, quiet evening together;

a simple dinner at a local restaurant with talk of school and troublesome clients and plans for an upcoming weekend. After dinner we strolled through the Barnes & Noble on 86th Street, randomly picking up books and scanning chapters. It was an enormous satisfaction to watch Elizabeth and Ava from afar, concentrated on a book, performing unconscious, characteristic gestures like Ava's rubbing the bridge of her nose, deep in thought; or Elizabeth, twirling a long strand of her chestnut hair as she read. We walked back down Lexington and at 84th Street we paused and hugged. The most natural thing in the world to me would have been to keep walking with them towards a shared home. But instead, they turned right towards Park, and I turned left towards the river. As I crossed Second Avenue I was bushwhacked by a surge of loneliness, accompanied by great gulping sobs.

Yes, that night it would have been better even to be here, in the study, than to be alone in my apartment. And so, with such shreds of consolation and gratitude to at least be under the same roof with the family I was trying to fit into, I finally drifted off to sleep.

Sag Harbor
Two-bedroom, two bath Cape on 90 × 100 lot. Wood burning stove. Deck. Water view. Walk to beach.

It seems I cried a lot in 1993. Or, more accurately, I would have surges of hope, punctured by worsening rifts with Ava. In June, Ava came out with me to Sag Harbor for an idyllic weekend of beach walks and lingering embraces. She loved the pattern of light the trees created on the simple white blinds of the bedroom. She cuddled close and talked about how we could fix up the place even cozier. We planned to spend ten days together in Sag in July when Elizabeth would be in camp.

In my naïveté, I neglected to realize that such a stretch of intimacy would be terrifying for Ava. Sure enough, she started whittling away at the vacation a week before it was to commence. Oh, she forgot it was parents weekend at Elizabeth's camp (from which I was excluded, *ipso facto*) and would be too tired to come right out afterwards. Oh, and some business connection would be in New York midweek, so maybe she would just stay in town and come out late Thursday, which transformed a ten-day vacation into a long weekend.

I decided to go to a gay foundation benefit alone the first weekend we had planned on being together; sort of an anniversary celebration of how we met.

Each summer in the Hamptons there is at least one upscale lesbian benefit at an estate by the ocean that attracts the professional class and trust fund babies of the community. While ostensibly it is to raise money for scholarships or legal work or health concerns of lesbians, it functions as a social gathering for schmoozing and a dating pool for the unattached. I went. I schmoozed. I danced a little. I decided to leave early and got my car stuck in the mud. I trudged back to the house to call my faithful AAA and could not read the small print on my membership card. I asked a young thing to read it for me, made the call, and waited. That night I became middle-aged; my eyesight falling to the need for bifocals. Bifocals before a baby. It was against nature. And Ava was no closer to making a genuine commitment than she had been years before.

Back in town a week later Ava engineered a two-hour session with her therapist for both of us. The nuggets I gleaned from the session were these: Ava was embedded in her family and would put them first no matter what they had done or would do to her. I was irrevocably an outsider. However, Jessica did see progress with Ava's time frame of movement towards a fuller relationship. She challenged Ava to proceed with actions rather than spinning scenarios. Jessica was also strong on the point that I *not* move into the Park Avenue apartment, but that we needed to get a new place, together, within the year.

I looked at Ava. Could a commitment to real estate be the key to the possibility of a sustained connection between us? I thought of her co-op apartment in Buenos Aires; the bedrooms she kept at her parents' homes in the suburbs of the city and in Punta del Este. Maybe there was another layer of truth here; I was preoccupied with her constant movement. But it was not random flight. It was more like continual motion from one rigidly maintained room of her own to another.

To be with Ava and to have a baby, would I need six cribs and an international diaper service? It seemed to be either that or become a single parent. With each moment of clarity with Ava came other complications for motherhood.

Mandate of Heaven

The Metropolitan Museum of Art was my secular house of worship. For most of my two-plus decades in New York, I lived within a short stroll of its sprawling presence in Central Park. It has answered my various passions through the years: Egyptian hieroglyphics when I was writing a novella on the Hypatia, the Neo Platonist philosopher from Alexandria; fifteenth century Sienese painting before and after my Italian journeys; Japanese wood block prints following a reading of van Gogh's letters to his brother; Romanesque architecture when my spiritual needs pared down from the too humanly confident Gothic; and the familiar pleasures of French Impressionism. Now, the Chinese galleries became my place of meditation.

Unlike other highly trafficked areas of the museum, this area was never crowded. I could stand in front of a scroll by the eleventh century artist Qu Ding, and lose myself in the mountain mists with never a jostle from another eager viewer. I'd sit in on a ledge of the Scholar's Garden courtyard of the Astor Tea House and take in the harmonious proportions of wood and stone and pond, watching the interplay of dappled shadows through the round moon gate and the skylight above that let in the natural light of day or glow of evening skies. Sometimes I'd sit on a bench in the cavernous hall of Chinese sculpture and think about how Kuan Yin, the goddess of compassion, filled the same need for all accepting mother-love as the Catholic Virgin Mary; or how the looming, handless sixth century Bodhisattva was so Christ-like (or was it that Jesus was so Bodhisattva-like?) in his choice to delay eternal bliss to aid humanity in its quest for unity with the godhead. I would sit, or stand, and think of a daughter born of this tradition, and how I could help her, connect to both this deep, rich vein of humanity and the rootless, anything-is-possible energy of America.

Ever since the intake interview at Spence-Chapin, and subsequent home study visit from the social worker at my apartment, I had been reading books on Chinese history and art; renting videos of *Raise the Red Lantern* and any other Chinese films I could find. I would eat even more often than usual at Chinese restaurants and quiz my friend, Mei Ping, about her life growing up in Singapore. Several times a week I would go down to the walkway along the East River and watch an old Chinese couple perform their early morning Tai Chi. Since Ava and I were on a trial "separation" for a month, I had more time than usual to pursue my Sinophile activities.

Despite the uncertainty about Ava, and my parents' declining health, I moved doggedly onward with the adoption preparation work; although through much of the fall I wove in and out of thinking I would truly go ahead with motherhood. Some days I would tell myself that there was too much going on, and that I should delay any major decisions until I felt centered. Or I would have a resurgence of my commitment to writing and the prospect of finishing a manuscript within the next six months became enormously enticing. After I accomplished that, I could think of a child again, I told myself.

On alternate weeks, I'd joyfully do things that would bring me ever closer to having a baby; such as getting six sets of my fingerprints done at the Sag Harbor Police station for the adoption application or making follow-up calls to a couple I had met with a Chinese nanny. On days when I had a midtown client, I would purposely take the route down the East River so that I could observe "my" silent, elegant elderly Chinese couple performing their morning Tai Chi exercises facing the water.

Much like a former party girl preparing to enter the convent, I also arranged pleasures for myself I would soon have to forgo if I became a mother the following year. I subscribed to the fall season of the New York City Ballet as well as the "short" season of the Met opera and toyed with the idea of booking a trip to Europe. I was going to do it during the Thanksgiving break but decided to put it off until Christmas when my friend Belle said she'd go with me if I could delay the trip until after her daughter's wedding in early December.

As the prospect of my daughter came more into focus, I also had to face the growing evidence that to proceed, I would be very much alone. The first ominous sign came in early September. Suddenly, on my morning walk by the river, I found only the Chinese woman performing Tai Chi in her customary spot. I looked for her husband that day and on other mornings, but he never reappeared. Then, towards the end of the month, just a day before I was to meet Ava for our reunion dinner, I noticed that the Chinese woman had moved her location, as if now that she was on her own, she got to pick where she would stand and gaze out over the water.

During the separation period from Ava I had composed what I thought was a thorough analysis of our situation and tucked it into my purse for presentation at the proper moment during our dinner. We met at a good fish restaurant near my apartment. She was lovely and wary. She was upset to learn of my father's recent hospitalization, "Darling, why didn't you call me?" she asked with concern.

"Because of our agreement," I replied, ever the good girl, following the rules.

"Ach, but this is different. I wish I had known."

"But Ava, what I would have wanted from you then was to *be* with you, have you stay with me. And I knew that wasn't possible."

"You know I can't stay there with your cats."

I nodded. No point saying that I could have locked them in the bathroom. I knew where the conversation was heading. She could not see her way to any actions that would make strides to uniting our lives, or even back to the way it had been. Friends. Maybe an erotic interlude now and then? No pressure on forward motion as a couple. Yes, that was the central message from her: No pressure. Of course, I could still see Elizabeth from time to time, especially when Ava was away on business trips. That would be good for her; normal. I was in tears by the time the main course was served. I never gave her my letter.

We played out this crippled connection throughout the fall. Dinners were infrequent, lovemaking sporadic and charged with the powerful alternating currents of reunion and farewell. The continual reunion and abandonment ritual was tearing me apart. In October, Ava called me weeping, declaring she could not go through with the separation idea after all and asked for a respite, to which I only too willingly agreed. A week later, when Ava was in Europe, I went to the Korda apartment to help Elizabeth with her Halloween costume. The entire class was to come as characters from *The Wizard of Oz.* In a wonderfully wacky way Elizabeth had decided on the concept of "Toto in the Snow" and needed assistance applying cotton balls to her dog outfit.

"You're an absolute blizzard!" I pronounced. "Come on, try it on. See if Kaiser Wilhelm barks at you."

While Elizabeth was changing, I circled around to Ava's bathroom to wash the Elmer's Glue and tufts of cotton off my hands. My eyes were drawn to the new addition of a row of framed botanical prints along the upper border of the long wall.

"Nice prints in your mother's bathroom," I said to Elizabeth back in her room after the Halloween fashion show. "Get them up in Connecticut?"

"No, I think the decorator got them for my mother. She's redoing the den and having a desk built into the wall and more bookcases and getting rid of the sofa bed so she can have a home office. You should see the cool new laptop she got."

I did my best not to look stricken in front of Elizabeth. Nothing was more final with Ava than a commitment to redecorate. She was moving on. Solo. It had taken me years to fully embrace the reality that Ava was not the destination in my life's journey, but a turnstile through which I had to spin on my way to full adulthood and a family of my own.

Ava confirmed the decisive ending of our coupledom after Thanksgiving, by phone. It was as if she wanted to finalize the issue before she and Elizabeth were to leave for their annual three-week stay in Punta del Este over the holidays, starting the following week. I no longer remember the words that passed between us during that call. The pain associated with it was so intense that I have blotted out the conversation. I do know that the comforting scrim of denial was finally stripped away so that on my way to Belle's daughter's wedding at the Stanhope Hotel on Fifth Avenue the following weekend, I dropped off Elizabeth's Christmas present along with the keys to the Korda apartment with the doorman of Ava's building.

Belle was a peach. Even though she was beyond busy as mother of the bride, she recognized the stunned silhouette of depression in my demeanor when she greeted me at the entrance of the long, rectangular room lined with chairs for the guests.

"Oy, it must be Ava," she intoned, shaking her head.

"Over. Totally."

"Good thing we planned Paris. You'll tell me everything." Belle nodded and squeezed my hands between her palms. "There's Bernie and Alice. You know them. Come on."

After Janice was married to her handsome half-Chinese boyfriend under the gaily festooned chuppah, we adjourned to a room upstairs overlooking the Metropolitan Museum of Art across the street for food and dancing. Belle made a point of checking back with me periodically throughout the evening and steering people towards me so I wouldn't try to drown myself in the punch bowl.

December was always difficult for me. I was one of those for whom the holidays brought more anxiety than cheer. Only one week into the month, and

Annunciation Window at Chartres Cathedral

the losses were piling up in record numbers. Ava and Elizabeth gone; not just to South America, but out of my cherished dream of family as well. My aunt Lu, my mother's sister, had died two days earlier, and my own mother was thrown deeper into confusion by the loss of her sister. One by one, the ladies of the Danube were fading from my life, to be replaced by…what?

I glanced out the bank of windows to the museum across the way illuminated by strong up-lighting and spots positioned along the roofline shining down on the ornate façade and steep bank of stairs up to the entrance. It was snowing. A heavy, soft snowfall that was not predicted swirled through the lights and laid a blanket of silent beauty over the city. The elegiac storm echoed the magic ice time I had shared with Ava in Connecticut the previous winter, and I mourned.

***

Two weeks later, Belle and I were on a tour bus approaching the town of Chartres. The spires of the Cathedral rose from the horizon, a fantastical apparition from a science fiction fantasy. The snow, which had started to fall as the bus left Paris, swirled in curlicues across the dun-colored stubble of an immense wheat field that lay between the highway and the town. Majestic was the word that leapt to mind. Not the dazzling opulence displayed at Versailles, where Belle and I had been that morning, but its somber sister. This was the place of soaring, sacred gray stone; the air a gusting tumult of metallic chill; this medieval dankness a mirror of my grieving heart.

My emotional condition had not improved since the wedding. If anything, it had worsened. Inner dialogs with Ava looped endlessly in my mind, along with replays of scenes footnoted for rewrites I would never get to re-enact. No stranger to the dynamics of hopeless attachments, Belle listened patiently to my ramblings for most of the flight. Despite jet lag, she was able to sleep when we got to Paris. I, on the other hand, spent the first night in the bathroom of our hotel room reading Flaubert's *A Sentimental Education* so that a light from the lamp and gulping sobs would not disturb Belle.

Our bus threaded its way through the town and parked below and to the side of the north façade of the cathedral. The moist snow dowsed my cheeks as I walked slowly up the rise towards the entrance. A deep weariness penetrated to my bones along with the moist cold. A few of the other tourists raised umbrellas in defense, dotting the cathedral's unyielding gray palette with splashes of red and yellow that relieved the severe, imposing beauty of the west façade.

My expectation of chill within the cathedral was pleasantly dispelled once I passed through the Royal Portal and stepped directly into the cavernous nave. The tour guide told us how fortunate we were to be there the week between Christmas and New Year, the one week the vast space was heated during the winter. We could take our time to explore the interior perimeter of the cathedral. I trailed the group as it wound its way counterclockwise through the nave to the south transept and on to the ambulatory. Halfway up the side, we paused in front of the Notre Dame de la Belle Verriere, the sole pane of stained glass that survived the twelfth century fire that destroyed the cathedral. It was the discovery of this intact window in the ashes that galvanized the faithful to rebuild the entire structure in an unprecedented brief period. Twenty-seven years is an eye blink in cathedral building terms; think of St. John the Divine in New York—it is still not done. Thus, the motivating power of chance and miracle, I thought, as I examined the famous blue glass of Chartres that made up the Virgin's garments and provided the backdrop for the attending angels that surrounded her.

From my reading, I knew that no tombs would be found in this cathedral. By the twelfth century, the cult of the Virgin had become a dominant force. Worshipped as the prime intermediary with her divine Son, cathedrals across Europe were raised in her honor, this being one of the most impressive and enduring. No tombs of the dead, only the promise of new life was to be celebrated here. For centuries women prayed in the side chapels before statues of the Virgin before facing the frightening and alarmingly lethal trials that comprised childbirth in the Middle Ages. I smiled to myself, remembering my mother's devotion to this feminine manifestation of deity and decided to send her a postcard from the shop I had spied, tucked into the North Tower near the entrance.

Then a rare impulse took hold of me. Prayer. Why not pray for clarity, for peace, for direction? Lines from T.S. Eliot's *Four Quartets* (which, for me, was a seminal text of my own spiritual canon) ran across my mind; lines such as "humility is endless" and,

"You are not here to verify, instruct yourself, or inform curiosity or carry report. You are here to kneel where prayer has been valid."

I was a tourist Catholic. In the United States I avoided churches, although after my first six months in AA, my anger had evaporated and mutated into benign acceptance of the kernel of truth that resided in all religions, regardless of the corrupting institutional carapaces they'd acquired over the centuries. By the late '80s, I could attend a wedding or funeral without gripping the pews until my knuckles turned white. My newly rediscovered spirituality learned to pray quietly amid my more dogmatically inclined neighbors. But in Europe, especially in the medieval cathedrals, I could feel the living spirit that transcended dogma and the chatter of theologians.

In 1984, during a trip to Italy, I first realized the power of spirit in man-made spaces. It was in Modena, the home of my grandmother on my birth father's side, that I had first felt the palpable presence of prayer layered through time. Up to that point I had entered churches as I would art galleries. It is as if there, in Modena, in the cathedral where blood ancestors had prayed, I finally understood that beauty flowed from spirit, and not the other way around. Three years later, when I found myself in the "miracle church" in Padua after I had been sober for more than a year, I no longer had trouble getting on my knees and praying. I actively participated in an entire Mass and even took Communion below a garland of crutches looped around the side chapels decked out like God's trophy room. I got on line with the other pilgrims to file by the sarcophagus of St. Thomas. Laying my hand on the cool stone that millions had worn smooth with entreaties, I spontaneously asked to be healed deeply through all the levels of wounds and slights I had tried to erase with booze and perfectionism. To my surprise, I burst into uncontrollable sobs as my palm cupped the stone. Be careful what you pray for. Healing is not for sissies.

Six years had passed between that visit to Italy and this one to Chartres. As the tour group moved out of sight around the back of the ambulatory, I remained standing in front of the window and attempted to still my mind with long, even breaths as I had been taught in Yoga classes. Empty the mind, I gently instructed myself. With the image of the Virgin, the Christ child, and six angels in front of me, I closed my eyes. Up from my heart, the single word "Help" rose spontaneously as my mantra.

Several minutes passed in stillness. I caught myself gently swaying and opened my eyes. With a nod, I turned and continued my slow course around the ambulatory, alternating my gaze from the exuberance of the sixteenth century choir screen on my left to the vaulting spaces and vistas to my right. And, always, the jeweled light through the windows.

As I approached the north side, I spied a woman lighting a candle in a small chapel that contained yet another Virgin and Child. A statue this time. How many years since I had lit a candle? Twenty, perhaps. Maybe more. Why not now? My mother always lit one if we were visiting a new church ... on vacation in Wisconsin or on a rare trip south... and always she chose to do so in front of a statue of the Virgin. A quarter or dime would be extracted from the coin section of her red leather wallet. Then into the slot. She'd pick up a long white taper and light it from one of the sputtering candles in the red votive glass and then ignite the highest candle she could reach.

"In honor of you, Mama" I said softly as I drew a five-franc piece out of my coat pocket and slid it into the tin box. It made a metallic click as it joined the other coins. Smiling at the woman who looked up at the sound, I brought the candle stub I found lying on its side near the coin box and dipped it next to a lit candle. Many of the candles had already burned down, but I found a half-full votive in the second highest row and reached to ignite the wick with my burning candle stub. I knelt, said "Please," and bowed my head as I had done as a little girl next to my mother on the soft-cushioned kneelers at St. Alexander's. Mother and daughter in lace mantillas my father had brought back from Madeira. Black and pink. Mother and daughter.

It was time to go. My tour group had completed its circle through the cathedral and gift shop. As I stood, I noticed that the woman who had been kneeling beside me was gone. Even heated, the cathedral was drafty. I drew my long shearling coat around me and walked slowly down the center of the nave, past the temptation of the north transept. Another time, I promised myself.

My eyes lifted to take in the entire west wall through which I had entered the cathedral. The huge West Rose window depicts the Last Judgment; Christ enthroned in the center, displaying his five wounds. Below the central window were the other shimmering survivors of the terrible fire; the three lancet windows of twelfth-century glass—that Chartres blue again!—that told the story of Christ in time lapse ... first the root of Jesse and those who prophesied the birth; then the Life of Christ, whose birth is announced to Mary by a green glass-winged Gabriel, and lastly, the Passion. Time running backwards in this view, chronologically forward on the way in.

I felt the stones beneath my feet slope and looked down. An immense labyrinth that mirrored the dimensions of the great West Rose above lay at my feet. Oh, yes, the guide had said that the nave was inclined to facilitate the cleaning of the stones. Pilgrims slept the night here. It was a refuge.

I raised my eyes once more to the windows. With strong sun, their brilliance would have studded the floor with liquid light. The muted, gray day kept the colors suspended above, intermediate between human and heaven. Then, to my astonishment, the entire wall appeared to vibrate as if a gentle force was breathing and the massive stone wall was the lining of a colossal lung and I a mere corpuscle swirling through the circulatory system of the cosmos. At the same instant I felt a tingling sensation creep in through my toes and feet, up my body, and out through my fingertips. My lips vibrated on the same wavelength as the wall that encased the transept windows.

A child broke away from his mother somewhere near the south tower and dashed towards where I stood, transfixed. The boy (or was it a girl? Bundled in a gray winter coat and stocking cap, it was difficult to tell) came to full stop five feet in front of me and stared, mutely up into my face. How long did we stand there, with the mother's voice in the background, calling? No way to know. The child became part of the pulsing luminosity of the moment. And then, deep from within my body, from a place behind my heart, a soft, strong voice rose to sound in my inner ear,

"A child wants to come to you," it said.

The mother finally walked up to her child and led him away by the hand. The child persisted in his focus, looking back over his shoulder at me with the same gentle smile while I returned his gaze, astonished. The moment his head turned away and he broke into a trot to keep up with his mother, the vibratory universe stood still. The tingle drained from my lips and hands. The massive wall rested in its ancient stone once again. I stood on the white stonework of the labyrinth, no more magical than a rubbed-out hopscotch pattern on the driveway of my own childhood.

And yet everything was new. From that moment on, never again did I waver in my course towards my daughter. Out of the ashes of grief I rose—no longer the one abandoned, but the one who took in the abandoned one, never wavering or looking back. Faith ignited my soul; there would be enough money; I would find help; I would be strong enough physically and emotionally to carry out parenting alone. I may never know the details ahead of time, but the message had been sent, delivered, and accepted. One day at a time, I would journey to meet the child whose cry had come to me through a holy winding circle and lodged, permanently, in the chambers of my heart.

The Middle Kingdom

At the end of June, I fell in love with a smudged, indistinct Xerox image of a baby girl with an abundance of dark hair surrounding a serious face. Magnifying glasses were of no use to bring her features into sharper focus. I dreamed into that piebald image and felt a new kind of love seep into my soul.

Her name was Lao Li. She was born December 1, 1993, along the Yangtze River in the ancient city of Wuhu, Anhui Province, in central China. She had been three weeks old when her spirit beckoned me in Chartres Cathedral during Christmas week. I xeroxed the Xerox, further dulling the image to get a copy I could carry with me everywhere and flash to anyone I could grab who would listen. I placed the "original" Xerox in a safe deposit box, the beginning of her ancestral archive. It would start with that paper. Like me, she would never have her original birth certificate with birth parents officially listed.

Francesca. Francesca Li Veto. I had been tempted to make her middle name Marie, like my own, after my mother. But I decided, instead, to give her a piece of her other heritage as part of her permanent name. That way, when she was a rebellious teenager, she did not have to go far for other options. I put everyone on notice that Franny was forbidden but allowed Chessy and Cesca as possible nicknames. Elizabeth persisted in her preference for Frankie.

I attended a preparation session at the adoption agency for the group who would travel together to China. There would be eleven of us winging our way halfway around the globe for seven babies ranging in age from six to eighteen months. The group would consist of three childless married couples and four single women, one accompanied by her mother.

There was a palpable difference between the couples and single mothers in the group. I came to understand that they had lived through a loss we single mothers had not. Prior to taking the steps to sit in that room, they had had to acknowledge that they could not conceive children of their own with their life partner. There was a layer of sadness and anxiety about them. We single mothers were just plain scared. All of us were euphoric. Pre-parenthood is a heightened state.

On one topic, I became the group harpy. The youngest among us quipped, "Well, one good thing is that by going to China we'll never have some birth mother knocking on our door wanting the baby back."

"The fact that my daughter will never know her other mother is *the* drawback of adopting in China," I blurted out. "I'm an adoptee and I found my birth mother when I was twenty-six years old, and it changed my life. I am sad that my daughter will not have that option. It almost made me rule out China. Birth parents contribute at least half of who are daughters will be, and to pretend otherwise is damaging to everyone, including that grieving birth mother."

The woman colored visibly, "I mean all those stories you hear, you know, with these open adoptions ..."

I did know what she meant, and I also thought that perhaps the pendulum had swung a little too far in the other direction since the days of my own secretive, sealed-record adoption. But the horse was out of the barn, and within the group I became somewhat of a cranky authority on the psychological pitfalls that might await our daughters.

The sun never set on the flight to China. We flew ever westward, in pursuit of the sun all the way to Tokyo, where we finally changed planes in midafternoon. I had slept only two hours, but I was not tired. The entire trip was one long meditation on parenthood. There had been so many arrangements to be made, so many details to attend to in the weeks leading up to the trip that I had not had time for reflection until then.

By the time we got to Beijing, we had finally caught up with the night. We descended into the stew of heat and smog that was summer in the Chinese capital and were met at the gate by Xiong Ying, the adoption agency's employee in China. Our group was among the first to adopt in China. Only 787 visas were issued for babies in 1994, in contrast to the 7,903 issued in 2005. By 2013, the number dwindled to 2,306 as China prospered and more stringent policies were put in place.

Xiong Ying never left our side for the next two and a half weeks, navigating the officials, airport, and hotel arrangements, and sightseeing for the group in her effortless, good-humored manner. We made our way to the hotel in a battered white minivan with our mountain of luggage stuffed with baby clothes, formula, and all the folding apparatus that attends Western infancy.

Bare-chested men fanned themselves on curbs lined with thousands of bicycles parked for the night. The heat was stifling and would remain so during our entire stay in China. Cots dotted the sidewalks of Beijing, some occupied by early sleepers escaping the heat of their small homes down the twisted maze of *hutongs* off the main thoroughfare. It was difficult to discern details in the quiet, deeply shadowed streets. I could only make out shuttered shops in the inky soup, punctuated by an occasional tiny, dimly lit noodle shop with a few slow-moving patrons.

Once at the hotel, we were back in the land of International Anywhere décor and the movie *Thelma and Louise*, in English, on the television. We were to have one day of sightseeing in Beijing before boarding an Air China plane to Hefei, the capital of Anhui province to the south. We had met as a group twice before our journey to be coached on preparation for the trip and, I suspected, to foster budding friendships. I rapidly formed a situational bond with Andrea York, one of the other single mothers who had a quick, very New York sense of humor that kept the group perky, even in our weariest moments. As a bonus, she had her mother with her, which was a comforting notion to all the first-time parents among us.

In the morning, Xiong Ying guided us across Tiananmen Square, through the Forbidden City, and then to a "Friendship Store," which was an official market open to foreign visitors. In the afternoon we boarded a bus that took us to a section of the Great Wall where we laboriously climbed to the top, traveled a span in the one-hundred-degree heat, and took pictures of each other with the winding wall disappearing behind us into the horizon, to prove that we had done it. Our day was a programmed bachelor party for parents-to-be. And while I'm glad to have had the experience, I don't think there was a person among us who would not just as soon have skipped the whole thing and jumped on the next rickety China Air flight down to Hefei and our daughters who, while we wound our way around the inner courts of the Forbidden City, were wending their way through country roads to meet us at the Anhui Hotel.

I chuckled to myself the next morning after we landed and made our way from the Hefei airport to the hotel in the middle of the provincial capital. Farmland, ocher and green: the Chinese Midwest. Francesca would be the third generation of women transplanted to the coastal life, though over the years I grew to appreciate how our native terrain defines us in indelible ways.

I took up residence on the fourteenth floor of the Anhui Hotel in Hefei with the other expectant parents. Andrea and I made sure that we were booked into adjoining rooms, which were mirror images of each other, with twin beds and a crib set up next to the window. After lunch, the babies would be brought to us in our rooms. We were to stay in the hotel for ten days to wait for the adoption documents to be translated before we could proceed to our next stop, Guangzhou, in the south, where we were to secure the exit visas for our new daughters. The wait was the proverbial blessing in disguise. It would give us the time to get acquainted with the babies and to practice diapering, feeding, and furtive napping before we had to take our act on the road.

I looked down fourteen floors through the yellow smog that permeated the sweltering city to the brown sluggish river that wound behind the hotel. There were fishermen casting their nets in lacy patterns on the ochre water and what appeared to be a public park on the banks of the opposite shore. It was difficult to know for sure. The smog was so heavy that that no horizon was visible.

"Can't we just call room service and take a nap?" asked Andrea as she cranked up the air conditioner.

"No room service. But the girl at the desk by the elevators will supply endless thermoses of hot water," I offered.

"Yeah, and tea, I bet." She shrugged. "What I wouldn't do for a Starbuck's."

"I brought some good coffee and a Melita filter. You're welcome to it."

Andrea flopped on to one of the twin beds. Her mother was exploring the gift shop in the lobby.

"And more bad news, Andrea. I think we better turn the A/C down, not up. These babies have never been exposed to it. Could shock their systems."

"Oy! I can't breathe this air! It'll kill us all!"

"Andrea, this is Central China, not Princess cruises."

"Oh." She blinked several times. "Gotcha. Hey, but I hear there's an Elizabeth Arden's at the White Swan Hotel in Guangzhou. Guess what the first thing is I'm going to do when we arrive?"

We went down to dining room to meet the others for our last meal as childless adults. One of women was gleefully trying every dish on the buffet, including the shrimp and other unidentified fish. She ended up retching horribly throughout her entire first evening as a parent. She was so sick that she tried to extract a promise from one of the other couples to take care of her husband and baby should she die. She survived, but the episode served as an object lesson to all of us to keep to the sticky rice, eggs, and green vegetables.

After lunch, we all went to our rooms to wait until 2:00 p.m. when the babies were scheduled to arrive. Xiong Ying said she would bring us our babies one by one. I sat for about fifteen minutes on the foot of one of the twin beds and surveyed my surroundings. I had designated one of the beds as a changing table and had the rice cereal and hot water thermos for mixing formula set up on the desk. And then, for whatever reason, I remembered the Catholic Charities office in Chicago and how meekly I had sat across from the social worker, trying to get information out of her about my own adoption, and suddenly I didn't feel like being such a dutiful good girl anymore. I got up and marched out into the hall and banged on Andrea's door.

"Xiong Ying?" asked Andrea as she flung open the door, expecting to receive her daughter into her arms.

"Come on," I ordered firmly. "Let's drag some chairs out into the hall. I want to be able to tell my daughter the whole story. I can't sit still in my room, just waiting for it all to happen."

"Hey, I'm with you!" Andrea swung around and waved to her mother. "Ma, I'll be out in the hall with Janine."

So, we sat, like old biddies on neighborhood porches, waiting for the drama to unfold. Two o'clock came and went. Andrea and I eyed our watches and each other.

First morning with my daughter, Francesca Li Veto, 1993, Wuhu, Anhui Province, China.

"Central China, right?" quipped Andrea.

"Yeah," I agreed. "I don't think punctuality is the priority here."

Just then we heard the phone ring in Xiong Ying's room and a quick conversation in Chinese. The door of her room, which was along the corridor perpendicular from where we sat, swung open and Xiong Ying hurried out to the opposite corridor near the elevators. Just as rapidly, she was back, leading a line of figures huddled over one, two, three, four, five babies swathed in blankets, despite the heat. The entire group was swallowed up into Xiong Ying's room before we had a chance to make out any of their features to see which ones matched the indistinct photos we all had been clutching for three weeks.

"Five babies?" I asked. "Where are the other two?"

"Just our luck that ours aren't here, right?" said Andrea.

They were not. For the next forty minutes we watched as Xiong Ying emerged from her room with one baby after another and turn right down the corridor to knock on one of the doors. One baby in a silver baseball hat and pink tutu dress was handed to a gleeful couple amid flash bulbs and clapping hands. Another one, an older child, wailed. Several were mute. One after another we watched the new families retreat into their rooms. All was silent in the hallway. Andrea and I still sat in front of our doors, crossing, and uncrossing our legs. "The Wuhu Two," as we had begun to call them, were nowhere in evidence. Another half hour passed. We were out of jokes.

The phone rang again in Xiong Ying's room. She threw open the door and nodded to us as she rushed to the elevators.

"They were waiting downstairs the whole time. They didn't know they were supposed to come up. I'll get them."

As she reached the elevators, the doors flew open and out rushed three adults, a boy about twelve years old … and our babies. Andrea and I jumped to our feet.

"Bai Yu," called one woman holding out at full arm's length the smaller of the two babies.

"Lao Li, Lao Li!" called the other woman, who immediately thrust out the other baby like a basketball poised for a hand off. The two women rushed towards us along the corridor. I saw my daughter's eyes shining like headlights on a car that was about to run me over and then, wham! She was pressed into my arms, wearing a red and white striped Snoopy t-shirt, Lady and the Tramp socks and a makeshift red cloth diaper. I gathered Lao Li/Francesca into my chest, dazed, and looked over at Andrea, similarly overwhelmed, staring at Bai Yu/Hannah, and jiggling her up and down. Our adoption pregnancy *pas de deus* concluded, Andrea and I turned away from each other wordlessly and exited into our adjoining rooms to process in private our moment of joy and awe with our babies.

From 3:00 to 4:00 p.m. on July 28th, 1994, I had my first hour alone with my daughter. I was nervous; was I holding her properly? Does my strange smell and look frighten her? How best could I reassure her that I was here to stay? Just shy of eight months old, she did not resemble the smudgy picture I carried. Her hair had been shorn close to her head so that she was almost bald. My searching gaze was met by her own stare of solemn intensity; Andrea was to dub her Nietzsche. She did not meet my eyes so much as concentrate on the top of my head, the first "yellow" hair she had ever seen. She was also drawn to light sources and any complicated pattern she could find on my blouse or bedspread, and, when tiring of these, she would examine her own hands methodically, turning them over and flexing them at regular intervals. Without toys, she had resorted to digital self-stimulation during the long hours in her shared orphanage crib where she was probably rarely picked up. God knows there was no bright mobile hanging over her crib nor the black and white cuddle toys so fashionable in New York baby circles that were supposed to help infants focus. And while she appeared healthy, I was concerned about her serious expression and wondered what I could do to put a smile on that smooth, lovely face.

Before going to bed, which was morning in the United States, I called my mother and father.

"What? You're in China?" marveled my mother. "What are you doing in China?" It was a bad memory day for her, but she was cheerful at the "news" that involved my becoming a mother and giving her another granddaughter. Papa was crying with joy.

The next twenty-four hours was a parade of firsts: I provided my daughter with her first solid food (rice cereal), put on her first diaper backwards and gave her a bath in the bathroom sink. She lost her "other" smell, but I kept her Snoopy T-shirt close by her crib so that her olfactory familiarity could be sustained a while longer.

That first night I lay next to the crib and poked my fingers through the blond wood slats to touch my daughter. I had been told that the babies customarily slept two or three to a crib in the orphanage, and I did not want her to feel the loss of body warmth so acutely. She did fall asleep finally, but I dozed only intermittently through that first night watch filled with tenderness, gratitude, and a shining hope for our future together. I knew firsthand, however, that no matter what grand good fortune came after, abandoned children are launched into life with a wounding loss that is physical, emotional, and psychic. I could not change that, but I could provide comforts and comradeship in the grieving when she got in touch with the darker side of the glowing life I wanted to give her.

I did not hesitate to show her the dual side of my own beginnings. I took her to Chicago many times those first years so that some direct memory of her grandparents would seep into her memory. My father cuddled her and made his Walleye fish faces for her and let his false teeth fall out for a laugh. He kept a photo of Francesca next to his bed the rest of his life, and I, in turn, have photos of him presenting flowers to her he had picked in his garden; another showing them gleefully blowing bubbles together and an assortment of others that demonstrate his persistent willingness to be a fool for love. My father died when she was not yet three, and Francesca's fourth birthday party was celebrated after the wake of my mother. My brother, his children and grandchildren, several cousins and my friend Virginia gathered in the dining room where countless family Christmas dinners had been served—and where Papa's hospital bed was set up during his final week the year before—to sing *Happy Birthday*. I looked out the window towards what had been a tiny pine tree my father, brother and I had planted in the center of the front yard when I was a girl and saw, instead, a towering pine. It was comforting to know that Papa's last earthly sight had been that tree and that my own daughter chased squirrels around its base. And most of all that there *was* that daughter.

While Francesca has only a hazy recollection of my Veto parents, she does remember times with both Evo and Bev. We made two visits to Evo and his wife Carol at their ranch house backed up to a golf course in Wimberly, Texas. The enterprising Evo created two restaurants and a new version of the Time Out Sports Bar in the Hill Country. Francesca enjoyed popping in at the Town Square Deli and Ice Cream Parlor to help clear tables and scoop ice cream. (Best part: the waitresses cut her in on the tips.) Always a promoter, Evo championed local bands and was instrumental in getting pro basketball established in San Antonio. He barely slowed down well into his eighties, but even Evo couldn't outdistance his failing heart. He died in 2012 and was buried with full military honors in San Antonio.

Introducing Francesca to Bev was emotionally more complicated for me. The first attempt failed, through no fault of anyone involved. Beverly had been poised to meet us on our return flight from China when we were to switch planes in San Francisco for the last leg of our journey back to New York. She and Randy had been living in Sacramento since the late 1970s after she had bottomed out with booze and Choco's troubles with the police in Manhattan. This would have been a wonderfully symbolic meeting, but it was not to be. A monsoon sweeping up from Tai Pei and an unscheduled refueling stop in Tokyo made us so late that Bev's oxygen supply ran out and she had to leave the airport and return to her apartment at the senior housing in Sacramento's Chinatown without meeting us. Decades of puffing Gauloise had shrunk her lungs to the size of fried bacon strips; never again could Bev travel outside the range of a portable tank of oxygen.

Randy and his wife Bridgett had kept the vigil, however, and were there on the other side of Immigration when we finally stumbled through, four hours later than scheduled. I hadn't seen him since he was a jive-ass teen in the late '70s when Bev had packed him off to stay with me for a week in Chicago. By the early '90s he was doing his best to straighten out and stay clean and sober after spending six years in Soledad State Prison for a rape he had committed at a drive-in movie while in a drunken blackout. He shouldered the large suitcase while making faces at Francesca in my arms, trying to get her to say, "Uncle Randy," while Bridgett—who was decked out like Jennifer Holliday in *Dreamgirls*—put her girth behind the smaller tote. Our ragtag caravan sprinted across two terminals and three flights of stairs to make a connecting flight to New York with only minutes to spare.

Francesca finally met Grandma Bev the summer she was six years old during a visit we made to friends in northern California. We drove from Berkeley to

Grandmother Bev with Francesca. Sacremento, 1999.

Sacramento and checked into the motel next door to the Wong Center, Bev's subsidized senior housing development on the edge of the capitol's Chinatown. I called Bev from the motel room to announce our arrival. She was waiting for us in the lobby when we walked next door a few minutes later after unpacking our suitcase.

"This," she announced loudly as she waved to the desk attendant when we were buzzed into the lobby, "is my daughter and granddaughter."

I smiled at the affable Chinese man and took Bev in my arms for a hug. Her thick hair had gone to gray and was cut in a semblance of a pageboy, giving her a weathered Prince Valiant look. She bummed a cigarette from the maintenance man on our way to the elevator, and Francesca obligingly greeted an elderly Chinese couple waiting for the elevator with a hearty "Nin hao." Bev beamed.

After an inspection of her studio apartment, we regrouped by the side of the motel swimming pool to give Francesca a chance to frolic. While Francesca slipped in and out of the water like a slender seal, my eyes shifted to the side of Bev's building. I counted five floors to find her west-facing window from which she enjoyed watching sunsets behind the horizon line of the freeway that blocked her view of the Pacific. And then I let myself imagine the moment two years earlier when Randy, giving up his struggle to stay clean and sober, leapt from that window. He had been coming down from a nasty crack high yet was composed enough to leave a suicide note and to wait until Bev went to the bathroom before flinging open the window in his rush to his final high. I reflected on how offspring of more famous characters who had done the same thing, who, by their action seemed to say, "I may have entered the world from your womb without my consent, Mother, but I will exit out your window on my own terms."

And then I heard Bev chuckle and nod her head towards Francesca spouting water from her mouth like a fountain.

"God, how could anyone give up such a child?" she said.

I caught my breath. It was a testament to how far along my journey I had come that my next reaction was laughter. A split second later the implications of what Bev had blurted out hit her as well and she joined in with a deep, hoarse chuckle.

As I dangled a clutch of pastel plastic keys above Francesca's crib that first night in China, I mused, "And where are your birth parents, my little one?"

It was unlikely that Francesca would have the same reunion experience that I had had with Bev, but with the advent of DNA testing, who is to say? There is not much I can do to improve on Marie Walton Veto's raising of me, but I do know that Bev's existence, the shadow of that "other" mother, was a source of anxiety for her which created a life-long zone of silence around the topic of birth mothers. It was as if she were afraid that the tyranny of blood could lay claim to me in a way she was powerless to counteract.

One night when Francesca was five years old, we were driving home by the beach near our house when she looked up at the stars spattered against the night sky and said, "Hello, China Mom. I miss you." She turned to me, "I want to know what she looks like."

"Yes, I know, my love. I felt the same way about my birth mom," I told her and gave her hand a squeeze.

"I'm sad," she said simply, holding my hand tightly as she turned her face back to the sky. And although there was pain in my heart for her, there was also joy that she could feel her loss and trusted me enough to share it with me with no thought of endangering our connection.

On the third day in Hefei, Xiong Ying knocked on my door while Francesca was waking from her nap and handed me Francesca's papers. Bound in white glossy paper covers, they were copies of the original infant examination record signed by three doctors, along with the English translations; a birth certificate, similarly translated, and a document translated as "A Certificate of Lao Li's Case."

Lao Li, female, was picked up on Dec. 4, 1993 at the area of the Laodong R. branch of the Public Security Bureau of Wuhu City. Having not found out her parents, the Baby has been sent to our Institute by the Laodong R. branch of the Public Security Bureau of Wuhu City. The Baby was name Lao Li. According to the doctor's examination, she is healthy. By her body's situation, we have drawn the conclusion that she was born on Dec. 1, 1993.

I burst into tears and laid the documents on the desk out of range of the bottles and coffee cup. Francesca looked up from her crib at the sound. I leaned over and scooped her up into my arms and sat on the edge of the bed and started to rock back and forth.

"I will never leave you," I said hoarsely, looking into the deep brown question in her eyes. "I will never leave you. I will *never* leave you."

Laid to Rest

Here is my eulogy scenario for Marie and Bev, Mother's Day, 2002, appropriately in May, the month of my birth and of my adoption. The morning light infuses honey highlights into the water as Francesca, a few friends, and I board the Staten Island Ferry. We visit amicably as we cross the harbor, then turn and head back to Manhattan. As we pull alongside Ellis Island on our left, I point out where my mother Marie Veto, neé Vlachovsky/Walton, first stepped on United States soil in 1908. She passed away in her sleep six years ago at the age of ninety-two in her twin bed in her American Midwestern home. The day of her death I stepped into the house of my childhood and found it transformed into a mourning chapel from the Old World. A score of Lithuanians, her care givers, and families, filled the house. Several knelt at the side of her bed, praying, as lit candles dotted the deeply shadowed room. As part of our tribute to Mama, I'd have Francesca hold an iPod with the sound of the Vienna Philharmonic playing "The Blue Danube" as I toss roses over the side of the ferry and watch them dip with the waves as if waltzing over the sun sparkled wake.

When we draw closer to shore, I turn my gaze towards lower Manhattan where Bev lived out her most idealized version of herself as a hip New York Village Beat writer/jazz fiend; part of the happening scene. Waltz tones segue to Miles Davis' "Kind of Blue" as I open the black shiny box containing Bev's ashes and scatter them to the wind, watching some billow out towards the open sea while a sudden gust drives a cloud of ash and bone landward to mingle with refuse encrusting the shore.

And what plays as we near the pier? Liza Minnelli belting out "New York, New York?" Or Aaron Copland's "Fanfare for the Common Man"? Perhaps... because there is something so American about this mongrel mélange of heritage and aspiration, blood bond, and new beginnings. My fantasy requires that my mothers fuse and comingle in the amniotic fluidity of the harbor to float the boat carrying my daughter and me. Francesca pipes up that she is hungry. We laugh, and I turn off the music. Our funeral party disembarks from the ferry and disappears down a Manhattan canyon for brunch.

Theoretically, this scene could have happened. Bev died in California at the end of February, 2002. Her niece Sue, who lived near Bev in Sacramento, informed me that when it was clear that Bev's lungs could not support her much longer they had had a frank discussion about Bev's impending death and arrangements that needed to be made. Bev told her, with a laugh, that she wanted her ashes scattered from the Staten Island Ferry.

"This is my piece," I declared immediately when Sue relayed the conversation to me. I called the funeral director in Sacramento and had them ship Bev's ashes to me in Sag Harbor. Several days later I retrieved a box wrapped in brown paper from the wisteria-entwined mailbox in front of my house. I placed it, unopened, on the lower shelf of my bookcase for several months not knowing what else to do with it. In spring, it seemed right to put Bev to rest. I started to make plans to deposit Bev's ashes in New York Harbor. I thought that Mother's Day would be appropriate but others I invited were busy, so I chose another Sunday in early June and started researching the logistics.

I soon learned that not only was it illegal to dispose of human remains from a public transport, I risked being arrested or at least detained and interrogated if I was observed flinging Bev, even in powdered form, overboard. Since September 11, 2001, New York Harbor had become the most tightly secured body of water in the world. Cars were banned from the ferry. Undercover agents were planted on each ship. Throwing *anything* into the harbor would have set off alarms of a nuclear or biological attack. Ironically, since the ashes of thousands of New Yorkers had fallen into the harbor in a nightmarish blizzard just months earlier, the addition of Bev's dust from a box the size of a Russian novel could have set off a panic of major proportions. Bev would have enjoyed the mayhem and subversive quality of such a melee and I was sorely tempted to give it a try.

Instead, this is the account of what actually happened.

I waited until the fall when the terrorist alerts in New York had lessened in intensity after the first anniversary of the World Trade Center attacks. Always one for symbolic gestures, I chose September 24, 2002, which would have been Bev's seventy-second birthday, for her ferry ride. I decided that it was too risky to try to conceal the bulky container and to dispose of the disconcerting bag of grayish powder and bone fragment it contained. I removed about two-thirds cup of the gritty, chalky ash and put it in a recycled plastic container that fit into one of my larger purses. Instead of making it family affair, I made the voyage with Susan, an old friend, who volunteered to go with me for moral support. It was Susan's savvy suggestion that we scope out the boat on the way over to Staten Island and to scatter them on the way back. That way, if we were caught, we would be detained in Manhattan rather than being stranded on Staten Island away from familiar terra firma and personal attorneys.

The sky was a serene blue above the glistening harbor as we boarded the ferry. We walked the length of the boat on both lower and upper decks as we chugged past the Statue of Liberty and Ellis Island and the more recent ring of naval cruisers anchored in the water close to the mouth of the harbor. We decided that the lower deck near the rear of the boat was the least populated and most protected from view. Sure enough, when we re-boarded the ferry at the Staten Island terminal, most of the passengers surged towards the front of the boat. I fancied that I saw the same cyclist that had accompanied us on the trip to Staten Island re-board as well and settle towards the rear of the boat, eyes scanning the crowd.

Once headed back towards Manhattan, I checked out the location of the cyclist I was convinced was an agent, and then squeezed myself into an area tangled with extra ropes next to the life boat to draw the container from my purse. Susan turned her back to me and tried to be as wide as possible while I pried open the lid. I thought it most fitting to read aloud the epitaph Gregory Corso, a fellow New York Beat who was born the same year as Bev, wrote for himself. Like me, he was the child of a teenaged mother who was given to Catholic Charities to be put up for adoption and found poetry as spiritual ballast.

Spirt
is Life
It flows thru
the death of me
endlessly
like a river
unafraid
of becoming
the sea

I said the words softly and tilted the container, letting the wind take the ash, like a tired puff of smoke that swirled then settled into the wake of the boat while the skyline of Lower Manhattan rose in front of us.

The rest of Bev's earthly remains resided with me for another month until my old friend Virginia from Chicago came for a visit in October. She had been at my side at the funerals of both my parents and, after more than twenty years of close friendship, was like a sister. The time was right to let the rest of Bev slip into the sea. I had learned that the current off the tip of Montauk flowed into New York Harbor so that Bev would have her wish in the fullness of time if I released her at land's end. Before we left, I impulsively removed a half-cup of ash and put it in a separate container back in my study. Bev had never seen my house by the bay but had once told me that she had always dreamed about ending her days in just such a setting.

While Francesca was at school, we drove out to Montauk for a lobster lunch, which was part of the ritual Virginia and I had concocted for the day. My cousin Sue in California told me that she and her father and son had been in the habit of taking Bev to Red Lobster for her birthday during the years Bev lived in California. Sue and her family had, in fact, marked Bev's birthday the previous month at the restaurant to honor her, the same day I had tossed her ashes from the ferry.

After our off-season lobster lunch, Virginia and I drove to the lighthouse and parked in the sparsely populated parking lot alongside the SUVs that belonged to surf-casting fishermen. We followed a path through the wind-tossed phragmites and gnarled beach plum to the rocky, narrow beach. I stepped out on to a rock, and after a meditative moment, tipped the ash from the container and watched the water turn smoky as it swirled around the rocks and trailed off toward the open sea. As I stood up, Virginia grabbed me by the elbow and pointed wordlessly to a lone goose flying past us, low, at eye level only ten yards from shore toward the lighthouse to our right and then onward towards the open sea.

"Peace, Bev," I whispered as the goose disappeared against the low hanging clouds over the water, the blue gray sky once again unpopulated and silent.

Three days later, after Virginia had returned to Chicago, I was in the dining room when our two rather large black dogs—Newfoundland and Lab mixes we had claimed from the ARF (Animal Rescue Fund of the Hamptons)—set up a polyphonic howl and rushed to the front door almost crashing through the full-length glass panel. Standing at the foot of the stairs was a large, grayish goose with one webbed foot poised on the bottom step. While ducks sometimes waddled past, and a neighbor kept chickens, this was the first goose I had seen in the thirteen years I had owned the house. No amount of barking or hand fluttering could turn her from the door. Finally, I put the dogs into their crates, grabbed an umbrella, and shooed the goose off the property. Ten minutes later, she was back at the front door. Once again, I unfurled the umbrella and banished her down the street towards the water with my flapping black shield.

This time I was taking no chances. Geese are tremendously social creatures. The fact that I had faced down two lone geese in the space of a few days told me Bev meant it when she said she wanted *all* of her to become the sea with none left behind as an ornament on my bookshelf. I grabbed the plastic container with the last bit of pulverized Bev from my study and headed to the end of my street where the water flowed out from a pooled-up pond, through Payne's Creek into the harbor and out into Long Island Sound.

"Rest easy, Mother Goose," I said as the dense dust sank to the shallow, sandy bottom and wisped outward with the current.

After releasing Bev, I climbed into my seven-year-old SUV to pick up Francesca at Sag Harbor Elementary School. I brought her home and fixed pizza bagels for her snack while she did her homework on the dining room table with Woody curled up under her feet. I kept an eye out for the goose, but she did not come back that afternoon, or the next day, or the day after that, either.

Finally, I turned back to the kitchen with Cleo, the ever-hungry Lab behind me, to make dinner and serve it to my daughter on the carefully preserved rooster plates I had inherited from my mother, Marie.

Our family, Sag Harbor, New York, 1995.

EPILOGUE
The Blood Garden
Autumn 2017

Our backyard, Madison, Wisconsin, 2017.

The Blood Garden

My yard has a cultivated border, an herb growing area to the side, and a wild native interior. When I moved us eleven years ago to take a job with the University of Wisconsin Foundation, I was pleased to find a purple lilac bush in the back corner, reminiscent of my childhood home in Villa Park, and a variety of evergreens and a majestic purple maple shading the back yard. I still smile when I turn up the soil to plant a new bush or perennial and pile up the rich, dark Midwestern soil teaming with twisting earthworms. This is true earth; the sandy soil of Long Island had always seemed anemic by comparison.

A rain garden of native plants was already in place at the back of the house, proudly performing its good citizen duty in holding back runoff to the nearby lakes and arboretum two miles downhill from our home. Here in the prairie lands, I learned the wisdom of native plants whose roots push down into the earth many times the length of what is visible above ground, holding the soil, preventing chemical runoff, making the plants resilient to heat and tumult of all kinds.

Now that I am retired, I have the time and inclination to spend more time reimagining the landscape to reduce the expanse of bothersome grass that just wants to be mowed. Thank goodness I have kept in touch with my cousin Kim since I met her on the Longwood's Iowa farm in the 1970s when Bev and my brothers made our first visit. I have been the beneficiary of her farm girl background and master gardener studies since she moved to Madison from Hawaii with her husband and youngest daughter last year. She taught me how to start seedlings in my basement with grow lights last winter, which led to a riotous first season experiment all over the yard. Kim likes to mix it all up: amaranth dye plants to the side of the front door next to the potted geraniums, begonia, and aromatic spurts of rosemary and lavender. In back, we reclaimed a square of land next to a patch of native flowers I had sown a few years ago and another patch to the side next to the herb garden. Kim went wild with tomatoes, round yellow cucumbers, eggplant, sunflowers, pepper plants, some herb varieties, garlic, turnips scattered promiscuously together with both annual and perennial flowers.

I blinked at this arrangement at first, having the orderly instincts of my mother, Marie, regarding combining edibles and bloomers, but grew to learn the fun of it all. Success was mixed. I take responsibility for the failures as I am the on-site partner with notoriously inconsistent weeding, watering, and harvesting habits. I do have seeds ready for next year—more prairie flowers and little blue stem grass, a line of sunflowers in front of the screen of arborvitae. To prepare the ground over the winter, I have put down old stained oriental-designed carpets. It looks like we are expecting Bedouins for Thanksgiving.

Francesca missed most of the growing season this summer. She was in Tianjin for three months doing a Mandarin immersion course for her major in Chinese language and culture. Her ruling passion is to speak perfect Mandarin. I understand. But even when I think I totally get it, she surprises me with her own hard-won wisdoms about her origins. The day of her jet-lagged return, when she was getting ready for bed in the middle of the afternoon, she was eager to display her most significant souvenir.

"Want to show you something, Mom," she said with a smile as she slipped off the blouse she was wearing over her camisole. "I designed it myself. I guarantee you that no one else has this tattoo."

I caught my breath. Running from the base of her neck to just above her shoulder blades was a heart overlaid with a triangle, surrounded by a seven-petaled lotus and an elegant swirl at crown and base.

"What?" I managed to sputter.

"The international adoption symbol, Mom. Don't you know it? I drew my own version and had it done in Beijing. See? The heart, the love that unites the three points of the triangle outside the triangle; you, me, and my China mom. They all meet up in the center of the heart. I added the lotus petals. The artist put in the squiggles."

Tears welled up in my eyes as I hugged her closely. Ah, how well I knew the desire to brand contested flesh. We citizens of the Adoption Borderlands chart our way across a blurry landscape.

A week later, Francesca came into the kitchen where I was washing tomatoes, laughing, and waving her iPhone.

"Ha, ha," she chortled. "I thought you were out in the garden, so I just went out to show you something and thought it was weird that your hair looked so dark from the back. But it wasn't you! I didn't know Kim was here. God. You two have the same hair."

It was my turn to laugh. "Yeah, I get it. We both have this riotous hair, but hers is darker, like Bev's. She looks more like Bev and I look like our grandmother. That's the way it dances out in the Phipps line."

"Yeah, and guess what. You know that 23andMe genetic test you gave me? I got a response! Looks like I have a cousin, too! Second or third, though. Look. Another Chinese girl from Wuhu adopted by a single white mom and living on Long Island! Three years younger."

Francesca scrolled down a Facebook page and handed me a photo of a lovely young woman with long black hair with her arm around her blond mother. Startled, I looked up at my daughter.

"Did you see this? Look at her hairline. It's the same as yours!"

Francesca leaned in to look more closely.

"Yep. Looks like it. Wonder what she's like. We've already texted. We're going to meet up when I go to New York at spring break."

In the continuing call and response of the adopted, we celebrate where we touch, what we can match, and what is our own.

"Yes, you must meet her," I say. "It's your birthright. Touch her."

You must touch her.

With Francesca at her University of Wisconsin-Madison graduation, 2018.

Acknowledgments

I am forever indebted to my friend Kaylie Jones and our New York writing group for getting me started on this book. Month after month we sat in her living room eating Pintalli's pizza and swapping drafts. Immense gratitude to Kaylie Jones, Tim McLoughlin, Nina Solomon, and Renette Zimmerly for your warmth and smart, generous feedback.

I would not have made it down the homestretch without my editor, Laurie Lowenstein. Her gracious guidance made this a better book than it would have been without her. Merry Anderson's careful reading and timely suggestions were invaluable.

Final proofing was done with skill and keen intelligence by Nadia Langley with my abundant gratitude.

On the production side, I could have no better partner than my longtime friend Charlie Grubb. With his gifted eye and outrageous humor, he is someone I always want to have in my corner.

Special recognition belongs to Virginia Smiley, writer and wit, who has shown up for over forty-five years, whether it's for the birth of a writing project, the death of a parent, lollygagging on beaches, or back porch sitting on the farm. Your friendship sustains me.

Author's Note

Janine M. Veto is the author of *Iris*, a novel, and has published poems and prose in journals and anthologies, including *Confrontation*, *The Dream Book, Fine China, la bella figura, Testimonies, Sinister Wisdom* and *Black Maria*. She lives in Madison, Wisconsin.

Made in the USA
Middletown, DE
07 April 2021